CAREERS FOR

FOR

FOREIGN LANGUAGE AFICIONADOS
& Other
Multilingual Types

VGM Careers for You Series

CAREERS FOR
FOR
FOREIGN LANGUAGE AFICIONADOS
& Other
Multilingual Types

H. Ned Seelye
J. Laurence Day

Second Edition

VGM Career Books

Chicago   New York   San Francisco   Lisbon   London   Madrid   Mexico City
Milan   New Delhi   San Juan   Seoul   Singapore   Sydney   Toronto

P
60.2
.U6
S4
2001

Library of Congress Cataloging-in-Publication Data

Seelye, H. Ned.
   Careers for foreign language aficionados & other multilingual types / H. Ned
Seelye and J. Laurence Day.— 2nd ed.
      p.   cm. — (VGM careers for you series)
      ISBN 0-658-01066-2 (hardcover) — ISBN 0-658-01067-0 (paperback)
      1. Foreign languages—Vocational guidance—United States.   I. Day, J.
Laurence.   II. Title.   III. Series.

P60.2.U6 S4 2001
402'.3'73—dc21   00–68497
                                                  CIP

VGM Career Books

A Division of The *McGraw·Hill* Companies

1 2 3 4 5 6 7 8 9 0   LBM/LBM   0 9 8 7 6 5 4 3 2 1

ISBN 0-658-01066-2 (hardcover)
       0-658-01067-0 (paperback)

This book was set in Goudy Old Style by ImPrint Services
Printed and bound by Lake Book

McGraw-Hill books are available at special quantity discounts to use as
premiums and sales promotions, or for use in corporate training programs.
For more information, please write to the Director of Special Sales, Professional
Publishing, McGraw-Hill, Two Penn Plaza, New York, NY 10121-2298. Or contact
your local bookstore.

This book is printed on acid-free paper.

Contents

Foreword

I'm pleased to contribute this foreword in fond memory
of H. Ned Seelye, a wonderful friend and colleague.

Today it was the Indian couple ahead of me on a flight to Denver speaking Hindi. Yesterday it was the television broadcast from Moscow, and the day before it was Hasidic Jews in Brooklyn. In each instance I got someone else's synopsis in English of what was happening. I may have gotten the facts, but I know that the real essence of the events escaped me. That inquisitive streak may be responsible for my interest in studying Spanish and in pursuing a career intertwined with the study of languages in addition to English by Americans. Contact with Mexican laborers, an elementary teacher who loved traveling in Mexico, missionary friends who lived and worked for years in South America, and finally a Spanish teacher who captured my interest and motivated me as no one had before—all this pushed me in the same direction. For me, an Iowa farm kid, this was all strange and unusual. But that was more than thirty years ago. Times and realities are changing.

In 2000, more Americans are studying modern languages in our public high schools than ever before—nearly 40 percent. What's more, they are studying an increasing variety of languages in addition to the usual French, German, Latin, and Spanish. Now it's Chinese, Japanese, and some Arabic; and Russian is growing again. One factor is instantaneous communication and the accompanying awareness of our world; but even more than that, it is the accommodation required of each of us, accepting and acting on the reality of our environment. Dealing with diversity has become a necessity of life, whether we talk of international politics, negotiations for foreign business, the retail business in many of our large cities, or simply understanding, appreciating, and getting along with our neighbors down the street. There is diversity at home and the wealth of language and cultural expertise that it provides. There is the push from Europe as it enters into a new era of cooperation in business, education, and all areas of endeavor. These developments have been brought into focus by the predominance of Japan and other Asian countries in the increasingly intense search for clients and markets.

But the essence of my message goes beyond earning a living. Language is integral to every aspect of life, whether it be our day-to-day routine or the enjoyment of leisure, travel, and the arts. We have traditionally thought of the knowledge of other languages and cultures as keys that would open doors and provide new opportunities. It is still true. But another important fact is becoming evident. The events that have brought us together, both here and abroad, also sometimes threaten to tear us apart.

Breaking down barriers of language and culture is a necessity and challenge that awaits and confronts each of us. We may pursue a career that utilizes this knowledge on a daily basis. Or we may simply require these insights and this knowledge to go about our lives. One thing is certain: knowledge of another language and culture will enhance your career—and broaden every aspect of your life.

C. Edward Scebold
Executive Director
American Council of Teachers of Foreign Languages

Preface

When this book first came out there were fewer than a hundred Internet websites in the world. Now there are hundreds of millions of websites. The information revolution has affected every aspect of our society. This new edition of *Careers for Foreign Language Aficionados & Other Multilingual Types* comes to you at a time when cyberspace and technology are changing the way the world functions.

While it is vital to adjust to the new reality, it is also important to recognize that technology is our servant, not our master. As Nathan Myrhvold observed in *The New Yorker*, "It is easy to get caught up in technomania and lose sight of the fact that communication, whatever technology carries it, is designed to link human beings." So here's the good news: proficiency in a foreign language is a greater asset now than it was when this book first came out. This new edition describes dozens of jobs for people who speak a second language.

You will learn about jobs in volunteer organizations, teaching English as a foreign language, working in major corporations with overseas offices, or working in foreign corporations with offices in the United States. Foreign language skills are needed in library and information science, social service, news gathering, entertainment, public relations and promotion, advertising and sales, medical and technical fields, teaching, travel and tourism, law enforcement, and jobs with the federal government. Translating, interpreting, teaching, and consulting are other career options. In this book, you will meet many successful people and read about how they got where they are and what they like (and don't like) about jobs that require two or more languages.

Do you love to play with English? Do you like to hear the sounds of foreign languages? Are you attracted to people who speak other languages and come from other cultures? Then you may want to find a career that requires foreign language skills. Are you good with words? Do you like solving problems? Would you enjoy figuring out how to help two people who don't speak the same language get together and meet their goals? Are you something of a mimic? Do you enjoy stand-up comedians? In *Mad Magazine*, do you like the strip "Spy vs. Spy?"

If so, you may be interested in the hundreds of jobs available for people who speak and write a foreign language. This book will give you some of the basics of this rapidly expanding field. You will be surprised, perhaps, at how many areas in our modern society require knowledge of a foreign language. You may also be surprised at how many career opportunities there are that combine the use of a foreign language with some other basic skill or talent.

You are aware that you are living in an information age, but you may not be aware of just what cultural and linguistic diversity there is in the information that surrounds you. Events of the past thirty years have brought changes in the way people work with each other, both within countries and from one country to another. New awareness of the value of differences in culture and language makes today's society rich and exciting. These differences can also be challenging, especially for those who don't have the cultural and language skills to deal with the new environment.

That's where you come in. With your language skills and your knowledge of two cultures, you can help people communicate with each other. You can help people get the things they want and avoid doing things that would be harmful to them. You can work with people and organizations to bring about true understanding.

You don't have to be a linguistic genius or a polyglot to find a good job and have a satisfying career using your second language. And the rewards of using your language skills are many.

A special feeling comes from helping people communicate with each other when they don't speak the same language.

Knowing a second language and being able to convey information accurately and appropriately in that language can build
one's confidence and self-esteem. Knowing another language
may also be the key component of an exciting and financially
rewarding career.

Some people have a gift. They seem to be able to learn other
languages quickly and remember vocabulary words easily. Other
people grow up knowing a second language because it was spoken in their homes. For these fortunate individuals, career opportunities abound, if they approach their goals with a clear plan
using accurate, up-to-date information.

This book is designed to help provide components for such a
plan and current career information for those who are already
well along the way to foreign language fluency. This book will
also be valuable for beginning foreign language students who recognize the great career potential that having a second language
promises. These people recognize that achieving fluency may
require considerable effort, but they feel that the rewards are
worth it. Whatever your career field or level of fluency, you can
probably find ways to use your language skills to advance your
career.

Beginning with organizations that accept and need volunteers
and moving on to service and sales positions, the book continues
onward to opportunities in teaching English as a second language.

Careers in commerce and business require specialized training
or experience in those fields, but knowing a foreign language
enhances the applicant's attractiveness to employers. Banking,
manufacturing, and consulting firms look for individuals with
business savvy and human relations skills. Adding a second language and cross-cultural training to those attributes strengthens
a resume considerably.

Information and service careers also demand language skills.
Careers in library and information science, human services, jour-
nalism and mass communication, and health care are covered in
Chapters 5, 6, 7, and 9.

People with a yen to see the world, as well as a desire to develop language skills, can find career opportunities in travel and tourism—a growth area in the coming decade. And there are jobs at home working for federal and local governments or as a translator, interpreter, or teacher. The next chapter will give you pointers on how to increase the likelihood of landing a job that lets you use your second language.

Acknowledgments

The authors would like to acknowledge the help given to them by Denise Betts, able editor for NTC/Contemporary Publishing Group, and by Lauren Brosnihan, Geri Chritchley, Chris Day, Stefani Day, Jerry Curtis, Lloyd Hudman, Chris Magerl, Duke Lambert, Lori Nickerson, Mary Helen Nickerson, Matt Nickerson, Tony Simmons, and Darlene Dean.

CHAPTER ONE

Jobs for Foreign Language Aficionados

Before we tell you about careers for foreign language speakers, we want to tell you this: there's a whole other world out there! Dynamics of the job market have changed dramatically. The Internet and the global economy have revolutionized the workplace. A decade ago, corporations, bureaucracies, and institutions were in charge of your career. Now you are. You define your aspirations and set your career goals by the way you package your marketable skills. And in today's diverse economic marketplace, foreign language is definitely a marketable skill.

Some people have a facility for languages while other people struggle valiantly to learn them. The easiest way to learn another language is to live in a home or in a country where that language is being used every day. You hear the same words and phrases so often that eventually they stick.

It doesn't take a genius to learn another language; little kids do just fine. Cantinflas, the immortal Mexican comedian, once told a good joke on the subject by observing that Americans are so intelligent. "I just returned from a visit to New York," he said, "and even children were speaking English there!"

Fluency in a foreign language is not only possible; it is increasingly beneficial. The world keeps getting smaller. It used to take a week bouncing around on the Atlantic Ocean to get from New York to Paris. Nowadays, an airplane will get you there in a few hours. Becausee it is so easy to travel now, many more people are doing it. Businesspeople, people visiting relatives, tourists—they all crowd the roads, railways, and airways. Increased travel means greater opportunity and incentive to learn foreign languages.

Those who do master another language find plenty of chances to use their skills. It makes travel easier and more pleasant. And with today's increased social diversity, people find themselves using foreign language skills closer to home, with neighbors and coworkers. Opportunities to use foreign language skills on the job are everywhere. And there are career rewards for all types of people who want, or need, to use a language other than their native one.

Develop a Plan

Before you go out looking for jobs, however, it is helpful to decide the level of foreign language skill—and skill in understanding how things are done in other cultures—that you are willing to develop. That decision will help you focus on the career choice or employment opportunity that you can realistically achieve. Then, what you'll probably want to do is set short-term goals that put you on track. Aim for a job where your language skills will be an asset. If you speak German, for example, find out about jobs in which knowledge of German will be useful.

According to *Forbes* magazine, the keys to success for promising employees, regardless of where they work, include a genuine desire to learn and communicate and the self-confidence to make mistakes. Respect for associates' backgrounds also contributes greatly to success. These same qualities also enhance one's ability to learn a foreign language. And fluency in another language, in turn, increases one's communication skills, self-confidence, and appreciation of other languages and cultures. Paul Aron, vice chairperson emeritus of Daiwa Securities America, was quoted as saying, "English is *an* international language, but it isn't *the* international language."

Given all the advantages, maybe you'll want to add a strategic language to those you already know. For example, one student, Alan, was raised in the United States in a Spanish-speaking home. This was neat because he learned one language at home and another—English—outside the home. In high school he began studying a third language—Russian—and enjoyed it. In college he majored in engineering but continued to take Russian courses as electives. After completing his engineering requirements, he went to Moscow to study for a semester.

Because he wanted a job that involved a lot of travel to other countries, he parlayed his fluency in three languages to get a job as an industrial engineer with a firm that had contracts in Latin America and the former USSR. Alan's job gave him weekends of scuba diving in Costa Rica, a chance to gaze at the Northern Lights in Siberia, and the opportunity to meet his future wife in Mexico.

Another student, Francisco, spoke Spanish and English at home, studied French in high school, and went on to major in Chinese at the university. Francisco's goal was to become a medical doctor and serve overseas with Doctors Without Borders.

If you enjoy learning from and communicating with people from diverse backgrounds, a career in which you use a second language may be just right for you. Let's look at some of the possibilities, beginning with those of easiest access and moving on to those that require more training but offer prestige and good salaries.

You may have learned a second language at home or at school, but it is obvious that language skill is aided by some kind of systematic training. However you learned another language, you will want to polish it through study. Nobody can say for sure which language will help you get a job. Most, if not all, foreign languages have some market value. In the United States, Spanish has become the dominant language in some cities and a strong factor in communities all over the country. French, German, Portuguese, Italian, Japanese, Chinese, Vietnamese, and Korean are helpful in certain positions. With changes in Eastern Europe and the former Soviet Union, and as economic, social, and political interaction increased, languages from those areas came highly into demand. Modifications of U.S. immigration policies and events in the Middle East and Asia have swelled the opportunity for employees who are fluent in languages from those regions. Francisco, the student mentioned earlier, hopes to be in the vanguard of a multilingual workforce.

Volunteer

Organizations of all kinds these days have connections and activities that spill over borders and across oceans. Civic, fraternal, educational, sports, professional, volunteer groups—all need secretaries and other clerical workers who know at least one language in addition to English. If you have clerical and organizational skills, and the basics of a second language, you can find immediate opportunities to use both.

You may have to volunteer your services to get your foot in the door. However, it will be worth volunteering if you improve your language skills and your understanding of organizations that have international connections. The chance to use your language skills, no matter how limited or undeveloped you may feel they are, is vital. You should recognize that being able to say a few words in your target language, or being able to recognize a few words written in another language, is a skill. And speaking a language is like playing a musical instrument: Practice is the key.

Opportunities to get that practice abound. Appendix A gives you information about state offices of volunteerism in all fifty of the United States and the provinces of Canada. On-line learning, televised classrooms, and home-study courses have revolutionized the way we learn. *Barron's Guide to Distance Learning* lists 250 institutions of higher learning that offer language courses that range, alphabetically, from Chinese to Swedish. More than one hundred colleges offer distance learning in Spanish.

The number of foreign language AM and FM radio stations has increased dramatically in the United States. And you may be able to enhance your language skills by watching a movie or soap opera in another language without leaving your house.

Other opportunities to improve your language skills can be found in every middle-sized to large city in America and, indeed, in virtually every town and hamlet as well. Just look at how many different languages are spoken in our own communities. In American cities, the number of languages spoken other than English often tops a hundred. Between recent immigrants and the many Americans who have foreign-born parents and grand-parents, the chance that there's someone who speaks your target language in your area is great. It takes some (but not much) effort to find those people, and it takes some self-confidence to approach them, but those are the very skills that you will want to develop for your career.

You should have a plan. How are you going to develop the skills that you need to succeed in a career using a foreign lan-guage? You may wish to start by getting a realistic picture of the situation you are in now and the resources you have at hand. You already know a little or a lot of some language other than Eng-lish. How can you improve your chances of using this skill to get a job? How can you improve your language skills? Do you have the funds to take language classes? Can you spend time with peo-ple who speak the language?

It doesn't matter what plan you have, as much as it matters that you *have* a plan. The plan should be logical and workable, and it should take you from where you are to where you want to be in manageable steps. Your plan should consist of steps that include using the tools you have to obtain the skills you need.

Three Keys to Success

Your chances for success will increase if you use three basic concepts as part of your career strategy: attitude, opportunity, and effort.

Attitude

The late Paul H. Dunn, speaker and author, told of going to a cafe in a small town. He asked the waitress what he should order for lunch.

She said, "Why don't you try our Enthusiastic Stew?"

"Why do you call it 'Enthusiastic Stew'?" Dunn asked.

"Because we put everything we've got into it," replied the waitress.

Succeeding in a career that uses your second language skills will require your enthusiasm. Enthusiasm is a way of looking at life. Steve Covey, in his book *Seven Habits of Highly Effective People* (Simon and Schuster, 2000), suggests that success comes to people who are proactive. That means they take action, rather that just responding to what happens to them. And they see things that happen to them as opportunities, even when such incidents appear to be negative. In your career plan, you should include an "attitude checker" that you turn on often to see if your thinking and attitudes are in line with your goals and aspirations. We all get discouraged sometimes, but maintaining a positive, proactive attitude is one key to success.

There is no perfect "type" of person who can succeed in fields where foreign languages are useful or required. Your personality can be whimsical, plodding, or analytical. What you need to do is build an attitude that will capitalize on your traits and make them work for you.

Opportunity

The Amazon River is one of the largest in the world. When it reaches the sea in eastern Brazil, the fresh water from the

Amazon flows far out into the ocean, beyond the sight of land. The story, probably apocryphal, is told of a sailing ship becalmed off the Brazilian coast. Crew members were dying of thirst. They signaled another ship, becalmed in the distance.

"Send us water."

"Let down your buckets where you are," came the signal from the other ship.

"Send us water."

"Let down your buckets where you are."

The thirsty sailors knew it would be fatal to drink seawater, but they did as they were told. They let down the buckets, and to their amazement and joy, the buckets came up filled with fresh water. The ship, though out of sight of land, had sailed into a patch of fresh water that the Amazon River had thrust out into the ocean.

Your career will prosper as you recognize the opportunities to further enhance and develop your second (or third) language skills. These opportunities flourish all around you. You simply have to let down your bucket.

Effort

As you prepare your plan and begin to build your career, be aware that you are the person who will set the level of the career achievement you wish to attain. It's a good idea to look at all goals as worthwhile. There are no "good" or "bad" goals as you move forward. There are no "high" or "low" goals. There are just goals. There are jobs and career opportunities that require little more effort than showing up for work and having a good attitude. There are career opportunities that require years of training, practice, and the development of specialized skills. The monetary rewards for the latter are usually higher than for the former. But you shouldn't consider only the prestige factors or the monetary rewards. As you make your career plan, think of what will make you happy and then evaluate how much effort it will take to achieve that goal. Plan to make the reward you want match the amount of effort you are willing and able to put into it.

For More Information

There are two great books that can help you develop strategies for getting a job abroad:

Krannich, Ronald, and Caryl R. Krannich, *International Jobs Directory*, Third Edition, Impact Publications, 1999.

Landes, Michael, *The Back Door Guide to Short-Term Job Adventures: Internships, Extraordinary Experiences, Seasonal Jobs, Volunteering, Work Abroad*, Ten Speed Press, 2000.

Canadian Job Sources

Young Canada Works: Get a job in a field related to your studies in a second official language. These jobs are for college or university students who can speak both English and French. Website: www.pch.gc.ca/ycw-jct/english/overview.htm

Youth Employment Strategy: Helps young people get the skills, knowledge, and work experience needed for a successful career (both official languages). Partnership opportunities for employers. Includes Youth Resource Network of Canada, a place to start to find your first job. Website: www.youth.gc.ca/YES

Council on World Affairs of Canada: This website contains important information and programs for students engaged in the study of world issues through United Nations activities. Website: www.cowac.org

CHAPTER TWO

Volunteer and Service Occupations

Mary Helen graduated with a degree in special education and taught for a while, then decided to change careers. She wanted to work with adults. She also wanted to go abroad. Mary Helen went back to college and obtained a master's degree in Teaching English as a Second Language. She studied Spanish but didn't speak it fluently, so she looked for a way to enhance her resume (changing careers had put her back to square one in the job experience category) and increase her Spanish fluency while she looked for an appropriate job. Mary Helen found a solution. She volunteered to serve as a social service missionary in Guatemala. She became part of a team that created a church-sponsored job-training center in Guatemala City. As a member of the training center staff, Mary Helen taught English, office practices, and basic computer skills. She worked mostly with working-class people who were trying to improve their job skills, but her English classes also attracted professionals from various fields.

Working with these people helped Mary Helen develop a specialized vocabulary in Spanish. More than improving language fluency, Mary Helen's volunteer duty helped her gain immensely valuable cultural insights and career-enhancing skills. Mary Helen's short-term goals were realized by her volunteer work. First she was able to list valuable teaching and professional experience on her resume. And, through using Spanish every day at the training center, her fluency improved markedly. When she returned to the United States, Mary Helen was offered a position teaching English as a Second Language and supervising orientation of newly arrived foreign students at a major university.

Does your career plan call for you to increase your language and cross-cultural skills before you enter the international job market or before you apply for a job that requires more foreign language skills than you currently have? If so, you may want to volunteer your services to one of the many community organizations or programs that work with people who speak your target language. They may need someone to help with correspondence, answering the telephone, translations, grassroots organizing, writing newsletters, doing research, or fund-raising. Sometimes these positions pay a stipend.

Volunteer Organizations

Volunteer organizations might include religious, government, or civic groups. The rest of this chapter is devoted to brief descriptions of these organizations.

Religious Organizations

Many religious organizations have relief programs and missionary programs that function overseas. Local congregations, even small towns, often have direct contact with people who live in other countries and speak other languages.

Many churches offer programs in their own communities for people who have immigrated to the United States. You might want to help in networking activities that help people find assistance for a wide range of problems. You may want to offer to teach classes for these immigrants.

These volunteer tasks will give you many opportunities to use your second language and learn about the target culture. Practice oils the tongue; it takes the squeak out of the voice and removes your hesitancy when dealing with people from other cultures.

Most congregations welcome your support and cooperation even if you aren't a member of the congregation. Typically, Christian church groups seek Christian volunteers of any denomination. There are exceptions, however. Jean, a high school student and professed atheist, was welcomed by the local Catholic priest to teach cooking skills to Hmong refugees. All profited from this exchange.

Government Programs

The Peace Corps employs more than 7,700 volunteers, all of whom must be trained in the language of the country to which they are assigned. This is a great program. Since it began in 1961, more than 155,000 Americans have worked abroad with the Peace Corps. Returning Peace Corps volunteers have found jobs in all kinds of agencies where knowledge of a foreign language and culture are valued. Your chances of getting accepted into the Peace Corps are much better if you have a skill that is needed by the participating countries. The Peace Corps looks for a wide range of skills in volunteers: engineering, medical, and teaching skills are always appreciated. The Peace Corps provides a great opportunity to learn and improve your foreign language skills.

If you would prefer to volunteer in the United States, you may want to consider VISTA. VISTA is the domestic counterpart of the Peace Corps. The organization seeks volunteers who know Spanish, French, or Indian languages.

The U.S. Office of Economic Opportunity also requires language skills for employees. It sponsors community action programs, such as Head Start, as well as legal services, health centers, and programs for migrant workers.

Civic Organizations

There are scores of organizations that have as one of their main functions interaction with people and organizations overseas.

Many organizations carry out local programs with specific countries and areas of the world. And different organizations in town may be working with different countries. So, in all likelihood, there is a club, fraternal organization, sister city or people-to-people program, or other group that is involved with local people or people overseas who speak your target language. Again, these organizations welcome efforts by members and nonmembers alike who wish to help. Some organizations provide stipends or scholarships to study or live abroad. Such organizations include Rotary Club, People-to-People, Amnesty International, Partners of the Americas, Lions Clubs, Kiwanis, and Sertoma. All are interested in promoting international understanding.

U.S. Civic Groups

Other U.S. voluntary service organizations are less well known. Here is a partial list.

ACORN
88 Third Avenue
Brooklyn, NY 11217

Volunteers must commit to serving for one year, and they receive a salary. ACORN prefers English-speaking applicants who also speak Spanish and who have prior experience in grassroots organizing. Work involves organizing low-income communities around issues such as housing, education, and health.

Los Niños
287 G Street
Chula Vista, CA 91910

This group focuses on community development and needs volunteers who can commit to one year. Program areas are school teaching, nutrition, family gardens, and literacy.

Casa de Proyecto Libertad
113 North First Street
Harlingen, TX 78551

The project seeks Spanish-speaking volunteers who have a knowledge of Central American politics to work with Central American refugees in detention centers.

General Convention of Sioux Indian YMCAs
P.O. Box 218
Dupree, SD 57623

This group needs volunteers with camp and/or community development skills to live in small, isolated Sioux communities and work on community development projects for between four and ten weeks.

United Farm Workers
P.O. Box 62
Keene, CA 93531
www.ufw.org

This organization looks for volunteers who can spend one year in rural or urban areas organizing farm workers or consumers.

And there are many, many other organizations. Some groups, like the five just mentioned, focus their efforts on people in the United States, many of whom speak little English. Other organizations focus on other countries, especially developing countries. Some examples of these groups follow.

Volunteering Abroad

American Friends Service Committee
1501 Cherry Street
Philadelphia, PA 19102
www.afsc.org

The group cosponsors six-to-eight-week summer projects involving construction, gardening, arts and crafts, and child care. Fluency in Spanish is usually required.

Amigos de las Americas
5618 Star Lane
Houston, TX 77057

The group seeks volunteers with at least one year of high school Spanish to work in health clinics in Latin America.

Brethren Volunteer Services
451 Dundee Avenue
Elgin, IL 60120

The group sponsors a wide range of community development projects in Latin America, the Caribbean, the Middle East, Europe, and China. Most tours are for one to two years.

Concern/America
P.O. Box 1790
Santa Ana, CA 92702

Hunger-relief and health programs in Bangladesh, Mexico, Central America, Sierra Leone, and the Sudan are the focus. The group seeks volunteers with a degree in public health, nutrition, agriculture, engineering, or medicine. Placements are for a minimum of one year.

Father Wasson's Orphans (*Nuestros Pequeños Hermanos*)
P.O. Box 1027
Prescott, AZ 86304

The group has orphanages in Mexico, Haiti, and Honduras. They need volunteers in construction, food preparation, and dorm directors. Placements are for one year. Room and board are provided.

International Voluntary Services
1901 Pennsylvania Avenue NW, Suite 501
Washington, DC 20006

The group sponsors projects in rural development (agriculture, public health, small enterprise, cooperative development, organizational management) in Bangladesh and in several Latin American and African countries. Placement is from two to three years. Room, board, and travel expenses are provided.

Operation Crossroads Africa
475 Riverside Drive, Suite 1366
New York, NY 10011
www.igc.org/oca

This organization operates self-help projects in community development. Knowledge of French is required for some of the assignments.

World Teach
c/o Center for International Development
Harvard University
79 JFK Street
Cambridge MA 02138
www.worldteach.org

This program sends college graduates to Africa, Costa Rica, China, Thailand, Poland, and other countries to teach for one year (usually in English) in secondary school. It costs volunteers about $3,500, but they earn a monthly salary of around $100.

NOTE: Most of these organizations operate with extremely low overhead. When requesting information of these agencies, it is a good idea to enclose a few dollars to help cover mailing expenses.

Other agencies include:

Peace Corps
1111 Twentieth Street NW
Washington, DC 20526
www.peacecorps.org

Habitat for Humanity International
121 Habitat Street
Americus, GA 31709
www.habitat.org

For More Information

Excellent sources of more detailed information on these agencies may be found in your local library; some are listed below.

Connections: A Directory of Lay Volunteer Service Opportunities
St. Vincent Pallotti Center
Cardinal Station, Box 893
Washington, DC 20017
www.pallotti.cua.com

Community Jobs
1516 P Street NW
Washington, DC 20005

International Directory for Youth Internships
Learning Resources in International Studies
777 United Nations Plaza
New York, NY 10017

International Workcamp Directory
VFP International Workcamps
1043 Tiffany Road
Belmont, VT 05730

Invest Yourself
Commission on Voluntary Service and Action
475 Riverside Drive, Room 665
New York, NY 10027

*Overseas List: Opportunities for Living and Working in
  Developing Countries*
Augsburg Publishing House
426 Fifth Street
Box 1209
Minneapolis, MN 55440

*U.S. Nonprofit Organizations in Development Assistance
  Abroad*
ACVAFS
200 Park Avenue South
New York, NY 10003

*Volunteer!: The Comprehensive Guide to Voluntary Service in
  the U.S. and Abroad*
Commission on Voluntary Service and Action
P.O. Box 347
Newton, KS 67114

Work, Study, Travel Abroad: The Whole World Handbook
St. Martin's Press
Council on International Study Programs
633 Third Avenue, Twentieth Floor
New York, NY 10017
www.ciee.org

Volunteers in Canada
Volunteer Canada
430 Gilmour Street
Ottawa, ON K2P 0R8
Canada
www.volunteer.ca

Volunteer Vancouver Center
#301 - 3102 Main Street
Vancouver, BC V5T 3G7
Canada
www.vancouver.volunteer.ca

Volunteer Centre of Winnipeg
410 - #5 Donald Street South
Winnipeg, MB R3L 2T4
Canada
www.volunteerwinnipeg.mb.ca

Recommended Readings
Goodman, Alan, and Fiona Smyth, *The Big Help Book: 365 Ways You Can Make a Difference by Volunteering*, Minstral Books, 1994.
Powell, Stephanie, *Careers in the Nonprofit Sector*, Harvard Business School, 2000.

A Word of Advice About Volunteering
You are following your plan to develop your language skills and launch yourself into an interesting, fruitful career. It is good to remember your overall goal at all times. It is also important to set short-term goals and to undertake activities that will help make

your long-term goals successful. To do that, you must really be interested in the people and projects of the organization where you work.

Remember to put the organization's purpose high on your list of priorities. If you approach volunteerism with a selfish attitude and think "I'll do this because I can see how it will help me. But I won't do that because that won't help me," you will probably not be successful. Think it through. Learn to accept assignments enthusiastically. Look for what is needed and begin to do those things that will help your group or organization succeed.

Rebecca had always been interested in Ethiopia. She hadn't had the chance to learn Amharic or any of the other languages spoken there, but she was willing to try. She noticed that there were lots of Ethiopian restaurants in a nearby city. After asking some questions of the people who ran several of the restaurants, Rebecca volunteered to be an aide in a preschool program that catered to Ethiopian children while their parents worked. After a year she had become functional in Amharic just from hearing it all day long from the children and their teachers. She was then invited to continue—as a paid aide.

Volunteering is an excellent way to improve your fluency and job experience, but you should choose an organization whose mission is truly important to you.

CHAPTER THREE

Teaching English as a Second Language

I n communities all over the country, new immigrants arrive to work and raise their families, just as our own parents or ancestors did. This continuing stream of immigration stimulates our economy and creates many opportunities for those who can teach English to speakers of other languages.

If you think you would enjoy teaching English as a second language, several options are open to you. Public and private schools at all levels need teachers. Businesses and community groups seek English as a Second Language (ESL) and English as a Foreign Language (EFL) teachers to help adults gain fluency in English. There are English language institutes, American schools abroad, and opportunities to tutor students privately. Whether you want to work with preschoolers or senior citizens, in the United States or abroad, there are always opportunities to teach English as a Second Language or English as a Foreign Language.

Preschool, Primary, and Secondary Schools

Our public and private schools often provide classes in English as a second language to students who have not yet developed sufficient fluency in English. This is a school's most common response to students who are just learning English. Many schools go even further. They offer bilingual education, teaching subject matter in the student's native language (so the student won't fall behind in science, math, and social studies) while also teaching English as a second language. Reading and writing skills are often taught in both languages.

Community Colleges and Universities

Most colleges like to have foreign students matriculate for two reasons. First, they enrich the campus social and cultural life, providing American students with broadening experiences of other cultures and peoples. Second, foreign students are a substantial source of income for the colleges. Foreign students generally have to pass an English language proficiency test (TOEFL—Test of English as a Foreign Language) before they are admitted to a degree program. Since many students arrive without the required level of English fluency, many colleges offer special intensive programs in English for these students so they can do well academically and participate fully in the life of the college. ESL courses offered to foreign students are frequently multicultural, with individuals from different ethnic and national origins enrolled.

Survival English

Adults in the community who are learning English as a second (or third) language have immediate needs that must be met quickly. Learning enough English to survive in the United States is one of the most important of those needs. Survival requires being able to communicate in emergencies to police, firefighters, health workers, and school administrators. It means filling out a job application and being able to read safety signs at the workplace. Survival requires skill in buying food at the supermarket, in using public transportation, or in getting a driver's license. For some immigrants, basic literacy is an immediate need.

These are the kinds of issues that ESL teachers focus on while teaching adults. These ESL classes are generally offered in the evenings. They provide a part-time source of income to ESL teachers, most of whom find the work exceptionally rewarding. It is fun to teach English to motivated adults from other lands. One Los Angeles ESL teacher put it this way: "These are special people, and they capture your heart."

English for the Workplace

The level of education for an average immigrant is several years higher than for Americans in general. Still, many new immigrants arrive with only a few years of primary education. Those without marketable technical skills, or well-educated immigrants lacking English skills, often find work in food service at restaurants or hotels. They may find jobs as taxi drivers or housekeepers. Wherever the work, learning English is usually an advantage.

Sometimes a corporation will offer ESL classes to its employees. These classes develop skill in using the kind of English that the workers need. Construction workers learn a different set of vocabulary from cab drivers. These ESL courses benefit both businesses and employees, and they may provide the perfect teaching opportunity for you.

English has become the international language of many professions: airline pilots and air controllers, businesspeople and diplomats. In many fields of study, especially technical areas, the only available textbooks are written in English. The result is that there are many people in the United States and other countries of the world who would like to learn some English in order to pursue their professions. This provides work opportunities for you if you would like to teach ESL, either in the United States or abroad.

American Schools Abroad

Most private schools abroad teach students English. Even American schools enroll students who are just learning English. The American School in Guatemala, for example, enrolls about 15 percent Americans; the rest are mostly Guatemalans. Of the 85 percent who are nonnative speakers of English, many are struggling with English. American schools abroad need dynamic people with experience teaching ESL. The schools generally require a teaching certificate from some state in the United States.

Investigating these teaching opportunities may be easier than you would think. When the authors typed "Teaching English Abroad" into the Google.com search engine, 133,000 entries popped up.

English Language Institutes

Every urban area of the world has privately run language schools, and English inevitably is one of the languages offered. Frequently, American tourists looking to prolong their stay in an interesting port of call will drop by these establishments and inquire into the possibility of employment. Usually the openings are for part-time teachers, and the pay is modest—barely enough to live on, if your needs are simple. But this is a wonderful way for you to meet people and get better acquainted with the country and to help pay for the experience.

The U.S. Information Service, associated with U.S. embassies abroad, often maintains binational culture centers in major cities. These centers feature libraries of English books, cultural events (plays, art exhibitions, lectures), and—most importantly—classes in English as a second language. Bruce had always wanted to spend a few years in Greece, and prior to visiting, he wrote to the director of the binational center there, enclosing a resume and indicating that he would be in the country for a visit on a set date and would call to arrange a meeting. Bruce not only got a job as ESL teacher, but things worked out so well that he became the center's director of curriculum several years later.

Finding opportunities in Greece (or Indonesia for that matter) will be easier for you than it was for Bruce. All you have to do is type "U.S. Information Agency binational centers" into any major Internet search engine. You'll see lists of overseas centers and a lot of other useful information.

Private Tutoring

Often people who can afford to will hire a tutor to teach them, or their family members, English. They find tutoring is a convenient way to learn the language. The tutor often goes to the student's home and teaches for an hour or two at a time, once or more a week. In some countries, this can provide a reasonable living for the ESL teacher. One ESL teacher in Tokyo, for example, has been teaching English to the same family for twenty years! One gets these jobs by advertising and through personal contacts.

Qualifications

Wherever you work, employers look for two major qualifications in ESL/EFL teachers. The first requirement is training in the techniques of teaching English to speakers of other languages. The other qualification is actual experience in teaching English as a second language. Both are important to your success as an ESL/EFL teacher.

Naturally, the more training you have, the more marketable you become. Some jobs, like those in colleges, generally require a graduate degree in ESL, sometimes a Ph.D. Most intensive English programs would like you to have experience abroad. Some insist on it. The jobs in public primary and secondary schools usually require state teacher certification. It is still possible, however, for someone with just a bachelor's degree to land a job as an ESL teacher. And jobs as teachers' aides generally do not require more than a high school education.

Often two or three years of experience teaching ESL are sought by prospective employers. This creates the classic dilemma: How do you get experience if employers want people who already have experience? As the singer Ray Charles puts it in one of his songs, "How you get the first is still a mystery to me." You can meet the catch-22 requirement for prior experience in several ways. Consider starting as a volunteer in a private agency's program (see Chapter 2), work as a teacher's aide, or plan to graduate from a program that includes a teaching practicum. John, an English major who enjoyed working with people from other cultures, wanted to learn Russian, but his college didn't offer it. During summer break at the end of his junior year in college, John made arrangements to work for room and board as an ESL teacher's aide in a summer program in the former USSR, gaining the chance to learn the language and experience the culture.

In addition to teaching experience and knowledge of ESL methods, sometimes two other qualifications are sought. They are knowledge of a foreign language and experience living in a second culture. ESL teachers can anticipate the specific problems their students may experience if they know the students' native language. For instance, if the student speaks Spanish, the teacher knows that the American "r" sound, and the "th" and light "i" sounds, will give the student some trouble. Sometimes it is not practical to speak the student's language because there may be twenty different languages represented in one classroom. Even so, to have experienced themselves the process of learning a foreign language helps teachers understand the students' problems.

Experience living in another culture is also helpful for ESL teachers. It improves a teacher's accent and increases fluency to use the language on a daily basis with native speakers. And knowledge of another culture can help the ESL teacher educate and understand students better. In addition, assignments abroad are easier to land if the employer knows that the teacher is comfortable living in other countries and enjoys experiencing a new culture.

For More Information

Sources of information on careers in teaching English as a second language are listed below.

National Association for Foreign Student Affairs (NAFSA)
Association of International Educators
1307 New York Avenue NW, Eighth Floor
Washington, DC 20005
www.nafsa.org

Center for Applied Linguistics
4646 Fortieth Street NW
Washington, DC 20016
www.cal.org

Institute of International Education
809 United Nations Plaza
New York, NY 10017
www.iie.org

TESOL (Teachers of English to Speakers of Other Languages)
700 South Washington Street, Suite 200
Alexandria, VA 22314
www.tesol.edu
(Most states and many foreign countries have affiliates.)

CHAPTER FOUR

Commerce and Business

T he Internet links the world as never before. Our planet has shrunk. It's now a "global village" where countries are only seconds away by fax or phone or E-mail. The Industrial Revolution of the nineteenth century flourished as technology provided commerce and business with rapid transportation and communication. Today, the world is in the midst of another titanic revolution—the Information Age. Part of that revolution, the Internet, is in its infancy, yet commerce and industry are now dependent on it. No industry is unaffected by it; every business model has been turned upside down and inside out by E-commerce. In these revolutionary times, being able to think "outside the box" will help ensure your continuation of employment. To be successful and advance in your career you must make yourself valuable to the company.

One way to make yourself valuable is to develop your language and cross-cultural capabilities because commerce has gone global. Business is conducted around the clock. Significantly, market power has shifted to consumers rather than manufacturers and business retailers. This new Internet economy needs workers who are cross-culturally aware and linguistically adept. The majority of employment opportunities are going to go to knowledge workers. Net-ready businesses need workers with creativity and enterprise as much as those with technical skills. Members of the new workforce will create, analyze, and disseminate information, and there is a huge shortage of skilled workers in the Information Technology (IT) industry. According to the Meta Group, there will be a shortage of 1.2 million IT workers by the year 2005.

Where will commerce and business find IT workers? Immigration is one place. Congress has adjusted immigration laws to allow entry to thousands of foreign workers to fill critically needed jobs.

Maria Schafer, a human capital management specialist, wrote, "A white-hot global economy driven by a high-powered technology engine is propelling IT jobs to the center of attention at organizations worldwide."

What does that mean to you, a foreign language aficionado with cross-cultural capabilities? It means that in your job, whatever it may be, you are likely to be working side by side with someone from another culture whose first language is not English.

As companies jockey for position in the marketplace, they seek clear, consistent, and continual communication between and among employees and management. With your language and cross-cultural skills you can be a valuable asset in your company's nonstop effort to build awareness and understanding of the company's culture.

Government regulations now require business and commerce to provide workers with time off for a variety of family-related matters. As a result, temporary/part-time employment and telecommuting have grown rapidly. According to the Bureau of Labor Statistics, some fourteen million people are employed in sales. Thus, in an ever-more ethnically and culturally diverse society, where temporary employment and sales jobs are flourishing, your linguistic and cross-cultural skills could help you gain employment and promotions.

Deeply involved with new technology is a breed of modern businesspeople who have a growing respect for the economic value of doing business abroad. In modern markets, success overseas often helps support and revitalize domestic business efforts.

Overseas assignments are becoming increasingly important to advancement within executive ranks. The executive stationed in another country no longer need fear being "out of sight and out of mind." He or she can be sure that the overseas effort is central to the company's plan for success, and that promotions often follow or accompany an assignment abroad. If an employee can succeed in a difficult assignment overseas, superiors will have greater confidence in his or her ability to cope back in the United States where cross-cultural considerations and foreign language issues are becoming more and more prevalent.

Thanks to a variety of relatively inexpensive communications devices with business applications, even small businesses in the United States are able to get into markets where the medium of exchange is the mark, the yen, the peso, or the pound. Large corporations have international branches or divisions, and they deal with foreign investors and buyers on a daily basis.

English is still the international language of business. The American dollar still talks clearly in the world marketplace. But there is an ever-growing need for people who can decipher another tongue. A second language isn't generally required to get a job in business, but having language skills gives a candidate the edge when other qualifications appear to be equal.

The employee posted abroad who speaks the country's principal language has an opportunity to fast-forward certain negotiations and can have the cultural insight to know when it is better to move more slowly. The employee at the home office who can communicate well with foreign clients over the telephone or by fax machine is an obvious asset to the firm. Such persons build a niche for themselves in the firm. They find they are included in the "loop" in which key company business is discussed.

Important Languages

According to a job service based in San Francisco, the leading languages that will be vital to U.S. business success in the next two decades are Spanish first, then Japanese, then French,

Chinese, German, and Russian. This research was carried out before dramatic political and economic changes took place in Eastern Europe.

Even more languages can be included in the list, and the order may be different depending on what business you are in. There are about twenty industrialized nations. These include Poland, Sweden, and Italy. Knowledge of Polish, Swedish, or Italian can be a real advantage to a businessperson.

Industrialized nations do not trade exclusively with other industrialized nations. They also trade with lesser-developed countries in Africa, Asia, and Latin America that nevertheless buy products from more economically developed countries. And, of course, it is easier to sell something to someone if you speak his or her language. Forcing the client to speak a foreign language in order to place an order with you puts you at a distinct disadvantage.

Asian languages are also vital to the new economic mix. The United States imports billions of dollars of merchandise annually from Taiwan, Korea, China, and Japan. And the entrepreneur with Russian or German or Chinese language skills—or the corporation with employees fluent in those languages—has a better chance than most of taking advantage of the expanding business opportunities in those parts of the world.

With so many choices, which languages should you study to advance your business career? Of course, the answer depends on your individual interests and aspirations. However, Spanish rates as the second language of the world, and, if you are looking for a career language that has high potential, Spanish may be it. Spanish can be easier to learn than some other languages because Spanish classes are offered in virtually every U.S. town, and you can easily find native speakers of Spanish to converse with. Demographic projections show that the percentage of native Spanish-language speakers will increase dramatically in the next two decades in the United States. With that rise in Spanish speakers will come an increase in the need for people who speak both English and Spanish and are comfortable with cultural realities of both societies.

Teaching Languages to Businesspeople

Business schools have begun to integrate foreign language requirements into their programs as they recognize the importance of language skills to their graduates' successes in the outside world. Some companies take the position that it is easier to teach a good businessperson a second language than it is to teach a language-skilled individual how to succeed in business.

That fact in itself offers career opportunities. Jobs and business opportunities are available for people who know other languages and can teach them effectively to business school students and business executives who travel abroad.

Setting aside for the moment the language programs of universities and colleges, there are many organizations that teach intensive language courses on a commercial basis. Some of these courses consist of ten one-hour sessions. The students learn grammar, usage, and cultural skills. Such organizations offer jobs and career opportunities for teachers, office personnel, and curriculum specialists who recognize the importance of cross-cultural understanding and nonverbal nuances in communicating with students.

Culture camps and workshops are another offshoot of the growing need for knowledge of foreign languages in commerce and industry. Language "cramming" is only part of the curriculum of culture camps. Other elements included are etiquette of the target society and dos and don'ts. This training makes it easier to move into target cultures without making a serious faux pas. Jobs at culture camps would be similar to those in language schools, but the camps put special emphasis on foreign cultural practices.

Job List

Following is a list of jobs in banking, manufacturing, consulting firms, and multinational corporations. Some of these positions require knowledge of a foreign language, but most do not. Even though the words "second language required" currently appear on relatively few business and industrial job descriptions, the realities of the business world strongly imply a need for language skills. It is up to you to take advantage of these implications and reinforce them through your own efforts to land a position or prepare for a career using your language skills.

You should also note that this list is by no means inclusive. For every industry, and for virtually every company, there are infinite variations of requirements and expectations. Even in jobs requiring the most basic skills, the ability to communicate well can be the key to advancement.

Computer and Information Systems

Almost everything we deal with these days is computerized—cars, television sets, microwave ovens, wristwatches, cash registers. The list is almost endless. The United States exports computers, computer software, and computer components. Thus, language skills are used in these positions:

Computer engineer

Information archivist

PC technical support

Independent consultant

Interactive media specialist

Intranet developer

Network architect

Telecommunications technician

Web business development specialist

Web content developer

Banking and Financial Services

Banking is the grandfather of international commerce. Banking executives and bank employees play well-established and long-standing roles in the field. What is new is the amount of bilingual and multicultural business coming into routine banking activities and procedures. In the following positions language skills can prove valuable:

Certified Financial Planner (CFP)

Loan officer

Private banking specialist

Financial services sales specialist

Advertising and Public Relations

The U.S. advertising business grew enormously during the economic expansion of the 1990s. The introduction of E-commerce advertising added depth and new dimensions to the industry at home and overseas. Opportunities in advertising will be more fully discussed in Chapter 7. But for the purposes of this business chapter, advertising positions break down into the following major areas:

Advertising account executive

Advertising copywriter

Graphic designer

Direct response marketing specialist

Special events marketer

Public relations manager

Environmental PR specialist

Human Resources and Employee Services

Whether in the United States or in the foreign division of a multinational corporation, human resources departments play a role of importance. Coordinating the needs and expectations of the company and employees helps move the company forward. Following are positions that are increasingly being filled by language-qualified people:

Benefits specialist

Human resources manager

Career counselor

International human relations consultant

Employee assistance program counselor

Research coordinator

Customer Care

All businesses depend on customer service employees who can handle requests of all kinds and take care of a variety of problems. Companies often depend on off-site specialists working with computers and telephone networks to provide this service with speed, accuracy and diplomacy. Foreign language skills are always an asset in these jobs. Following are positions in customer service:

Receptionist

On-line customer-care representative

Product support specialist

Web sales representative

Manufacturer's representative

Product service consultant

The lists in this chapter just break the surface of jobs available in business for people with language skills. Banking, retail, manufacturing, and advertising have all gone multinational, and many require second languages of their employees.

For every position mentioned, dozens more exist or are being created. And while knowledge of a second language may not be a prerequisite to employment, having a foreign language can make you stand above a group of monolingual job applicants. The best advice in the business area is to get a specific skill that you are interested in following as a career, and take steps to learn a language that will enhance your value to the company.

The best strategy usually calls for getting a job with a U.S. firm that does business abroad, then positioning yourself within the company for an overseas assignment. That way you get paid in dollars at what is usually a higher salary rate than that paid for comparable jobs in the host country.

CHAPTER FIVE

Library and Information Science

At a nearby library, the staff used to watch for the pickup truck that always came during lunch hour. The passenger stayed in the truck, listening to the radio and eating lunch. The driver went straight to the second floor of the library—to the computer room. He stayed for fifty minutes working diligently at a terminal. Then he returned to the truck, and the two drove off, apparently returning to work for the afternoon. A library staff member confided he would like to know what the computer was used for on this daily occurrence that continued for a long time. But, says the librarian, it would have been an invasion of privacy to attempt to find out. This story points out important attributes of the public library system. A vast array of information is available at the public library in a personal and private work space. It is true that we live in the Information Age.

The depth and breadth of human knowledge is expanding at an amazing rate. So much new information is produced around the world each day that it is impossible to keep track of it all. Information is power. Those with the technical and artistic skills to sift through this glut of data and extract the relevant tidbits required by a client or employer are increasingly rare finds and, therefore, are more and more valuable to many employers. This is the expertise of the librarian and the information researcher.

Libraries exist in all parts and levels of our society and go by many names: media centers, electronic databases, archives, and information centers. A library by any other name is still a library: a storehouse of information.

This information can be stored in many formats that go beyond the traditional bound book. Electronic storage utilizing computer technology is becoming more popular, convenient, and efficient.

The usefulness of multiple language skills will depend on your job title and the type of library where you work. There are basically four types: public libraries, school libraries, research libraries, and special or corporate libraries. The particular language skills required will also depend upon what specific area you work in within the library organization.

Types of Libraries

Understanding your attitudes toward your work environment is very important when considering a job in library service. Library types are defined by the community that they are designed to serve. Corporate and research libraries are highly structured, and the information needs of their users are often very technical and demanding. The parameters often are highly specific and detailed and often come with deadlines and cost restraints. School and public libraries, on the other hand, are far less demanding of technical skills but will require a more people-centered approach.

In all types of libraries and all facets of the job, computers are playing a larger role. Anyone contemplating a career in library service or information science needs to be comfortable with computers and other information technologies. Because of the rapid advances and upgrades in this industry, you must also be adaptable and trainable. A technical understanding of computers is not necessary, just a familiarity with computer applications and a willingness to learn more. Within the library profession, there are ample opportunities for both technically minded and people-oriented personalities.

How your language skills will help you, and what expertise is required on the job, will be more precisely determined by the area of the library you work in, by the opportunities that arise, and by the effort you expend.

Training

Whatever job you perform in the library world, it is important to get training in library skills and information management. On the job is a good place to start, to see if you like the work and to acquire basic knowledge. Many colleges and universities offer elective courses in library use and bibliographic instruction that would be very valuable. High-level jobs and employment at research libraries generally will require a master's degree in library and information science.

All library jobs fall into one of two categories: patron services or technical services. Those in the first category work directly with the community. The key responsibility here is reference service.

Patron Services

Reference librarians deal directly with the library users and help patrons locate the information they desire. In public and school libraries, this requires good human relations skills. Technical perfection in a second language is not as important as being open to foreign language patrons at the library and understanding their needs. Certainly basic conversational skills are paramount. And developing basic reading skills in another language enables a librarian to find the appropriate book or magazine for a patron—even if the vocabulary of the material itself is beyond the librarian's capabilities. Here, too, a feeling for the culture beyond words and verb conjugations is a valuable asset.

Many libraries seek to expand their offerings to include titles in the native languages of their clients. Chris, a librarian in an inner-city grade school, calls Spanish-speaking people in the area for leads on books written in Spanish that children enjoy. She also attends book fairs to get ideas and occasionally visits a Spanish-speaking country on a book-buying tour.

Library administrators are looking for confident, open employees to staff their reference departments—employees who are comfortable with people regardless of their ethnic or language backgrounds. If you are a "people person" who is willing to use your language skills—however halting and rudimentary—to communicate with patrons and successfully help them find the library materials they seek, you will be a valuable addition to a public or school library staff.

Reference work at a research or corporate/special library requires a much greater fluency in foreign languages and higher-level library-searching skills. Where the information sought at a public library may consist of a good book or a consumer report on used car quality, the information needs at research and special libraries are usually far more technical and exacting. A broad vocabulary in all your acquired languages is a must in order to understand patron queries and provide accurate answers.

If working in reference or in special libraries interests you, plan on extensive educational preparation. In university research libraries, it is routine to require one or even two foreign language proficiencies for a reference position. In addition, an advanced degree in library science and a college degree in the specific subject within which you will work is required. Your undergraduate work should include developing an understanding of the technical vocabulary within your subject specialty.

Your chosen subject specialty will often dictate the language proficiency that would be most useful. Any foreign language fluency can be useful, but for some specialties certain languages are more helpful than others. For example, if you have a bachelor's degree in chemistry and wish to work as a science or reference librarian, German, Russian, and Japanese would be more useful to you than Polish or Portuguese. If you work in literature or economics, Spanish, French, or Chinese might be more applicable than Bahasa Indonesian. On the other hand, if the library caters to a community of Portuguese- or Indonesian-speaking people, then this would not be true.

Because reference librarians at these larger or more specialized libraries can also be asked to translate material for patrons, the most advanced language proficiencies can make you very useful and valuable. Translating articles or technical manuals within a research discipline requires the most fluency and technical skills of any library language assignment.

Technical Services

The second category of library work is technical services. Here, librarians work with the information materials directly— whether they be books, paintings, movies, exhibits, or electronic data. They work to categorize, catalog, and organize the materials to make them readily available and accessible to the community. These jobs do not require the interpersonal communication skills that patron services do. As in reference, different levels of language ability can be useful in the technical services area.

Acquisitions

Acquisition of material is an important technical service. This department selects material for purchase. Prescreening of foreign language material may only require a rudimentary understanding of another language, enough to make the librarian capable of recognizing a good review in a literary publication in that language. When materials arrive in the library, someone must decide what department should receive them. This is not as simple as it might sound, particularly in the case of materials published or produced in a foreign country.

Research libraries, in particular, receive materials from all over the world and not just materials that support the teaching of foreign languages. In assembling a reliable collection on any subject, there are important contributions made in many languages. When this material arrives at the library, someone needs to identify what language it is in and what subject area it deals with. This could best be done by individuals with a broad familiarity with languages, but neither fluency nor even basic communication skills is needed.

Materials in foreign languages purchased by public or school libraries are not as far ranging. Foreign language needs are dictated by the community the library serves. It is important for employees in both technical and patron services to have language skills that reflect the demographics of the local community. In the United States, the single most important second language for a public or school librarian is Spanish, though obviously in most urban areas there will be concentrations of languages from all over the world, and any second language skill will be valuable in major metropolitan areas.

Cataloging

The second major technical service is cataloging. To be a cataloger in a research or special library requires an advanced degree in library science. This is also where the most language expertise is required in technical services. Catalogers need to be able to identify the key subjects addressed by the material and then accurately describe it both in the language of the library in which it appears and in English or the principal language of the library. This requires a broad vocabulary, and, like reference service researchers, library catalogers usually specialize in one or more subject areas. This means they must have the expanded vocabulary requisite for their specializations. Though technical accuracy is a must, written and verbal communication skills are not necessary. All of a cataloger's job is reading and writing, so proper accents and vocal nuance are unnecessary.

If you are interested in being a part of the Information Age and have a bit of the private eye spirit in you, your second or multilanguage skills can be put to profitable use in library and information science. If you like to find the needle in the haystack, the *Stecknadel* in the *Hauhaufen*, the *aguja* in the *pajar*, and the *tsahts'ósí* in the *tl'oh*, this could be the job for you.

For More Information

American Library Association
50 East Huron Street
Chicago, IL 60611
www.ala.org

American Society for Information Science and Technology
1320 Fenwick Lane, Suite 510
Silver Spring, MD 20910
www.asis.org

Canadian Library Association
328 Frank Street
Ottawa, ON K2P 0X8
Canada
www.cla.ca

Special Libraries Association
1700 Eighteenth Street NW
Washington, DC 20009
www.sla.org

Library and information studies programs can be found at www.ala.org/education.

Employers will often list jobs with schools in their geographical areas. A list of accredited program addresses and phones can be requested from the American Library Association.

Newspapers can be another good resource. The *New York Times* Sunday "Week in Review" carries a special section of ads for librarian jobs in addition to the regular classifieds. Other large city editions often carry job vacancy listings in libraries, both professional and paraprofessional.

CHAPTER SIX

Human Services

One interesting professional area with employment opportunities for people with language skills is the field of human services. Like health care professionals, human services workers come into contact with people who are poor, unemployed, victims of child abuse, homeless, or in poor health. The work settings can be as diverse as group homes and halfway houses; correctional centers; mental health facilities; family, child, and youth service agencies; and substance abuse programs.

While jobs for social workers do not pay especially well, the job outlook calls for a faster than average expansion in the number of jobs available through the year 2005. One area of growth, for example, is in services to the aging.

Another area of human services is recreational services. Jobs in the area of recreation are expected to grow about as fast as those in other areas of the economy. Recognition that in many areas many clients speak little English will make it easier for qualified people with language skills to find jobs in the field of human services.

Other sources of jobs are private and government organizations that help immigrants and other people with limited fluency in English get along in the United States. These groups require employment counselors, caseworkers, and supervisors who speak the languages of their clients. Opportunities for social service careers are not limited to major cities where immigrant populations tend to be large. Many immigrant people live in widely dispersed areas of the country. They are found in all regions and states, in big cities and small towns.

There are positions in social work that involve working with employment records, resumes, legal documents of all kinds, and correspondence with social agencies abroad. This work requires people who are able to decipher foreign languages and tease information out of odd-appearing documents.

Job Requirements and Challenges

As with positions in the health care professions, social work positions tend to be "people intensive." They require you to be interested in helping others with a variety of social needs, from education and employment to individual personal and family matters. If your career plan includes some kind of social work, you will want to study the ways in which language skills and human skills combine in this area. You will, as in the case of volunteers discussed in Chapter 2, want to focus your efforts on making things better for your clients.

You will want to familiarize yourself with the regulations and requirements of the social agencies and organizations you represent. You will want to identify potential problems that these regulations and requirements might pose for your clients who speak a language other than English and who may come from a cultural background different from your own.

Such potential problems may not lie just in the differences in language. If people have religious, dietary, social, or political customs or beliefs that conflict with the regulations of your agency or organization, you may be the only person who can solve the dilemma. And to solve it, you will have to understand the regulations involved as well as the cultural reality that controls your client.

One example of a cultural tradition clashing with the tradition of a social service agency occurred in Chicago as a state agency attempted to provide group health and education counseling to a tribe of Roma (Gypsies). The way the agency organized the group sessions offended these Gypsies' sense of propriety. The agency had proposed that the groups be divided into age levels. The Gypsy leaders were horrified that grandchildren were to be separated from their grandparents and equally upset that males and females were to be together in the same class. The counselors in this case proved to be flexible, and a simple compromise solution was agreed upon—to divide the classes by sex but not by age. Social service work often demands the ability to make such compromises.

Social Work

Social workers generally help people who are having difficulties dealing with circumstances in their lives. There are many kinds of social workers. The major areas of social work practice include child welfare and family services, mental health, medical social work, school social work, community organization, planning and policy development, and social welfare administration. A bachelor's degree is usually the minimum academic requirement to work in these fields. Often a master's degree is required. A social worker's effectiveness in helping people who do not speak English is mightily aided by a knowledge of the client's native tongue.

Frequently, the needs of someone from a particular country can be anticipated by a knowledge of the client's culture. Many people from India, for instance, are Hindu. Among their religious practices is a proscription against eating meat. It would be helpful, therefore, to be able to identify area restaurants where good vegetarian food is served—not just fruit salads.

Community Affairs

Planning

If you have organizational skills, you may want to work with people who plan activities that focus on, or seek participation of, ethnic and linguistic groups in the community. These activities may be anything from a large-budget annual observance, such as Spanish-American Heritage Week, which is put on for the whole community or region, to a picnic for preschool children in a small ethnic neighborhood.

It is difficult to overemphasize the need for knowledge of the cultures involved as well as sensitivity to the social hierarchy of the target community. You may have to check with people about what kind of colors to use in the banners and bunting, what sort of food and drink would be appropriate, and which dates to plan events and which dates to avoid holding certain activities. Your advice on the type and location of sites for the events may also be needed.

Communication

This work involves, among other things, getting the English language mass media—newspapers, magazines, radio, and television—to be aware of, and involved with, the cultural and linguistic groups in your community. It also involves writing, public speaking, and identifying other individuals in the target community who are good spokespersons.

There are many levels of positions and job opportunities in community affairs planning and community affairs communication. They range all the way from people who work at setting up and carrying out the activities, to people who plan the activities, to people who have overall responsibility for planning and coordinating all cultural and linguistic efforts that the community undertakes.

Sometimes it is difficult to find any long-term residents of a community who speak the language of the most recent residents. There are towns in Minnesota, for example, that have become home to sizable numbers of Hmong immigrants, a mountain tribe of farmers from Southeast Asia. Making effective contact with them has required identifying a network of human resources in the state that could help inform social workers about Hmong customs, aspirations, and problems. People who could speak Hmong were needed to assist in the initial contacts. One successful community affairs planner not only set up a good network of people who could contribute something to the needs of the Hmong; he also made arrangements to have local Hmong tutor him in the language. This was widely appreciated in the Hmong community.

Home Health Aides

Many social services consist of helping people who have had health or emotional problems and now need home visits from time to time to monitor their progress and give them assistance. It is hard to help if you can't understand the client's language. And an appreciation of the person's culture can also help in providing health care.

A sizable community of people from the Dominican Republic resides in a town in New Jersey. With what most temperate-zone Americans would regard as minor changes in temperature, many Dominicans feel a cold coming on. To help them feel comfortable in their new homes, one successful home health aide provided them with an orientation that included how to identify cod liver oil and where to buy it. In syrup or pill form, cod liver oil is widely taken in many parts of Latin America as a cough remedy.

For More Information

Further information on job openings in the field of human services may be available from state employment agencies or from city, county, or state departments of health, mental health and mental retardation, and human resources.

For additional information on careers in human services, you may want to visit the websites of the following organizations; contact names and addresses change annually with the election of new officers:

National Organization for Human Service Education
www.nohse.org

Council for Standards in Human Service Education
www.cshse.org

CHAPTER SEVEN

Journalism and Mass Communication

M edia and communications industries are good places to look for jobs and career opportunities. Much of the world is moving to the Internet, and you can get in on the ground floor of the Information Revolution. Historians compare our times with the social, political, and economic transformations that the invention of printing and the Industrial Revolution created.

Mergers in the 1990s created complex communication organizations. For example, Time, Inc., a magazine empire, merged with Warner Bros., a motion picture giant, to create Time Warner, Inc.; Cable News Network (CNN) was added later to form a magazine, movie, cable television behemoth. America Online merged with Time Warner to create one of the largest communications conglomerates in the world.

Some people see these developments as the triumph of technology over humanity, and fear that jobs will be lost and people will be shunted aside as the Internet economy flourishes. Many experts paint a more positive picture. They say that the new technology has created an unrelenting need for content. The Internet's need for people with skills in writing, video, animation, illustration, photography, and music will grow. The people who write, animate, illustrate, and take photographs will have to be managed.

The Internet culture is not self-managing. It is a human artifact. People who can manage visual, technical, creative, economic, and political transactions, many happening in real time, in cross-cultural settings, will be in demand.

Job and career opportunities are abundant. The problem is that the Information Revolution has given them labels that don't fit the traditional communications/media job profiles. Newspapers and magazines are still delivered to your door, but they are also available on-line. Jobs for word people may be listed under labels such as corporate communications, community communications, training and development, or even video game design.

Early in the computer age, most typewriter companies saw themselves as manufacturers of machines. IBM saw itself as a word processing organization. When typewriters and the companies that made them went the way of buggy whips, words were still being processed abundantly at IBM. Management experts like Tom Peters say that the new environment puts people, not corporations, in charge of their careers and their lives.

You ought to think of yourself in terms of the skills you possess and not how well you might fit a specific job description. You can tailor your skills and capabilities to fit the career path you decide to follow.

The publisher of the *New York Times* put it this way: "I don't give a tinker's damn how we distribute our information. I'll be pleased to beam it directly to your cortex." Sometime in the future the *New York Times* will cease to be produced on newsprint by roaring presses, but you can bet that the Times organization will still be in the information distribution business.

As you consider a career in communication, remember that multinational media companies are developing and marketing media products abroad, and they want to staff those offices with people who can speak more than one language and understand cultural differences.

Print Media

Until the world switches entirely to electronic information technology, you'll still find a wide range of job opportunities within traditional print media organizations, including book, magazine, and newspaper publishers.

Book Publishing

Thousands of new books are published each year. Take a look at any traditional or on-line bookstore and see for yourself. And nearly as many will be translated for markets overseas or translated into English for the U.S. market. Publishers need a variety of people in a number of positions to read and translate manuscripts. Here are some of the standard jobs in book publishing:

Author

Acquisitions editor

Audio book abridger

Book buyer

Book marketer

Book packager

Book reviewer

Fiction editor

Freelance writer

Rare book finder

Copyeditor

Designer

Publisher

Translator

As you can see, the job opportunities in book publishing are diverse. Books are beginning to be published directly on the

Internet, as well, which involves additional skills. Most jobs require a combination of language skills and some other talent, such as artistic, sales, or writing ability. If publishing interests you, plan to develop both your language skills and another specialization. For example, designers need a background in art, and promoters often study marketing. And many publishing professionals take continuing education courses designed specifically for those in the field.

As in all fields, work experience is the best way to test your interest and aptitude. Internships, entry-level jobs, and freelance positions provide great on-the-job training and a good introduction to the world of publishing. You can locate potential employers through numerous search engines on the Internet and through the reference desk at your local library.

Magazines

Magazines originally developed from newspapers but have since nearly swamped the publishing world. Using better paper, more color and photographs, and a different writing style, magazines have constantly evolved to suit the needs and whims of society. Now, specialty magazines cover every conceivable subject, from cats to monster movies, from log homes to modern science. And many specialty magazines have begun to serve the needs of people with a second language. Here are some common positions on a magazine staff:

Staff writer

Acquisitions editor

Contributing editor

Copyeditor

Design and layout editor

On-line magazine editor

Columnist

Photographer

Freelance writer

Researcher

Editorial assistant

Art director

Artist

Circulation/subscription manager

Because magazines offer diverse job options and cover a wide range of subjects, you should be able to combine your skills and interests in seeking a job in this field. Jobs for editors and graphic artists have increased dramatically. Competition for jobs in magazine and book publishing, however, is stiff. However, skill in a second language can help make you more marketable. You should plan to combine your language skills with other specialized education and as much job experience as you can develop before seeking your first full-time job in publishing. Major cities such as New York and Chicago are headquarters to many magazines, but technology has made it possible for staffers to work at home or in distant offices.

Newspapers

Many of the jobs at a newspaper are similar to those at a magazine or a publishing house. The main differences between newspaper and magazine work are writing styles and content. Newspapers generally focus on timely newsworthy events, possibly going into depth on a topic over a period of several days of daily publishing. Magazines, by their nature, allow longer deadline periods that lend the writer more time to dig into a story, develop it, and deliver it in a polished form.

Newspapers have access to the worldwide news-gathering capabilities of the Associated Press as well as foreign news services such as Reuters and Agence France-Presse. Nevertheless, when important news breaks abroad, newspapers may send their own staff reporters to the scene. This is particularly true when the news event affects the local area directly.

Staff reporters chosen for these short-term overseas assignments are, first, good reporters. Secondly, they are often persons with language or cross-cultural skills. Often the language the reporter speaks may not be the language of the area where the news event is taking place, but local editors often perceive individuals with language skills as qualified for assignments anywhere abroad.

The increase of on-line and free newspapers has created more jobs. Creation of positions for graphic designers, Web masters, and circulation sales and promotion personnel, among many others, has widened the field of jobs available in the newspaper industry. The increasing number of small-town and suburban papers, combined with the high turnover rate in the industry, will provide new jobs for journalism graduates. And language skills will give you a competitive edge, especially if they are combined with a degree in journalism and experience on your school or local paper.

In addition to using language skills abroad, local reporters will find opportunities to speak their target languages while investigating a news story or writing a human interest piece that involves people with little or no fluency in English.

Electronic Media

Radio

Radio has changed dramatically over the years. It began as a medium of the spoken word, became a medium of sophisticated entertainment programs—including comedy, drama, game, and variety shows—then was gradually overshadowed by the rising star of television.

Formats changed, listeners changed, but radio continues to grow. What car on the road is complete without a radio? What home doesn't have a radio in every bedroom or living room? All oldies, all rock, all gospel, all talk, all news—all these formats are in use and flourishing across the nation.

Talk radio has become the fastest-growing format in radio; half of all American adults listen to an hour of talk radio a week. One of the most dramatic changes in radio came at the beginning of the new century. Early in 2000, the Federal Communications Commission announced that it was setting up hundreds of free, low-power radio stations for nonprofit groups across the country. The FCC wanted to increase the diversity of voices on the airwaves. People were invited to submit requests for a license, and 750 requests came in for the two hundred or so licenses in the first ten eligible states. According to the *New York Times*, the FCC envisioned as many as one thousand micro-stations, each with a broadcast range of seven miles and with a combined audience of millions for an entirely new group of broadcasters. This could be the biggest change in the radio industry since the growth of FM in the 1960s. Many of these stations will beam their broadcasts to foreign language listeners.

Another major change in the radio industry is its availability over the Internet. One example is EyeQ radio (located on the Web at www.EyeQradio.com), which is based in Miami but runs audio programs from all over the country.

All-Spanish stations are common in the western states, and the government still beams foreign-language programming into hundreds of countries, including Russia. Jobs abound in radio for people with second languages. Although the skill generally is not required for employment, in most cases there are those positions for which a second language is a prerequisite. Here are some of the jobs you could pursue:

Commercial station manager

Micro-station manager

Talk show host

Advertising manager

Business development director

Local/national sales representative

News announcer

News reporter/writer

Promotions director

Traffic/continuity manager

Engineer

Producer

Public service director

Like the other communications careers, radio is a popular field. It tends to attract more people than can find employment. So although the Department of Labor expects average job growth through the year 2000, competition for positions at radio stations can be keen. Most find that it is easiest to get a start at smaller stations outside the major metropolitan areas. Pay for these positions can be low, and many aspiring broadcasters work in small towns for years before getting a chance to go on the air at a larger station.

Television

Television is the most powerful mass communication medium in the world—it combines near-universal and instantaneous delivery of sound, sight, and motion at no cost to the viewer. No other medium can do that. And television delivers local as well as national and international content. Broadcast television in the United States is currently a mass medium whose success depends on delivering one hundred million households to advertisers of products used in every home. But cable, computers, fiber optics, and the Internet promise to give consumers much more control over what they view. One cable executive predicted a five-hundred-channel universe.

Major manufacturers of home entertainment and information products now offer receivers that deliver digital-quality audio-video and instant software downloads to personal computers. Such networks can deliver customized media information and entertainment to the desktop computer via digital TV broadcasting, thus combining the efficiency and immediacy of broadcast with the customization and control of the home computer.

The need for program content will be enormous. The flow of programming between nations is predicted to rise as European and Asian nations produce their own giant conglomerates to compete with those in the United States. The growth and development of television means jobs at home and abroad, at all levels of the industry. The array of jobs in television includes:

Station manager

Sales personnel

Program director

Promotions director

Producer

Technical director

News announcer

News director

Videotape and digital editors

Graphic artist

Website director

As you would imagine, most of these jobs require specialized skills and training unrelated to foreign language fluency. However, as the number of Spanish-language and educational stations increases, fluency in a second language will be a special asset in this competitive field.

Foreign Correspondents

The largest and most affluent news organizations have overseas bureaus staffed by foreign correspondents. The reporters who work for these prestigious organizations are among the best reporters in the world. Back home, highly trained, often linguistically and cross-culturally trained editors receive their material. Executives of these organizations, if asked, say that their overseas bureaus are staffed exclusively by individuals who worked their way up from news operations. Because the number of media with established foreign bureaus is limited, and it may take a good reporter a decade to get abroad, many people are dissuaded from aspiring to a career in foreign correspondence.

They needn't be. There is another way to become a foreign correspondent: going abroad as a freelancer. Freelance correspondents work for themselves anywhere in the world. They sell news and feature stories to a variety of news organizations in various media—broadcast, print, and Internet.

According to Al Goodman and John Pollack, authors of a book on freelance correspondence, the companies that provide news and entertainment programming are the big winners in the television revolution. They envision more communications growth as the Internet continues to diversify and integrate the world of information. Anyone with a computer and a modem can publish on the Internet. Microsoft chairman Bill Gates wrote that he expects citizen-driven communications to sweep the world as communications costs come down and a critical mass of localized content becomes available in different countries.

In the stressful conditions that foreign correspondents often encounter, strong communication skills are a must. Not only are they important for your own comfort and safety, they are an essential part of doing the job well. The correspondent's duty is to report the facts as completely and accurately as possible. In order to do that, a journalist must be able to understand his or her sources and the subtleties of the language they speak.

In addition, it is helpful for foreign correspondents to attain as much knowledge of and sensitivity to other cultures as they can. Such awareness often makes it easier for a journalist to gain the confidence of sources and hosts in another country. Understanding the culture is just part of the job.

If you're interested in becoming a freelance foreign correspondent, an excellent investment would be the book *The World on a String: How to Become a Freelance Foreign Correspondent* by Al Goodman and John Pollack (Henry Holt and Company, 1997).

CHAPTER EIGHT

The Entertainment Industry

I n recent years, mergers of huge companies have brought news, entertainment and business organizations together in conglomerates that promote each other's products while competing among themselves for consumer dollars. First, Time became Time Warner, which then acquired Cable News Network (CNN). This giant merged with America Online to become a multi-everything behemoth. The creation of these huge corporations makes the United States competitive in the global marketplace. Having the muscle to compete globally gives the United States the power to maintain its dominance as a producer of world-class entertainment worldwide.

The United States has exported entertainment and culture for more than a hundred years. From early silent movies to television series to jazz to Cabbage Patch Kids promoted in the shadow of the Great Wall of China, U.S. creativity and marketing have been the envy of competing countries.

The U.S. cultural consciousness has risen significantly in the past quarter century. In the old days, U.S. entertainment entrepreneurs behaved culturally in the way nineteenth-century colonial powers had behaved politically—with little regard for the social, cultural and linguistic implications of their actions. Twenty-first-century entertainment giants must take all aspects of the global market into consideration. And multilingual, cross-culturally trained individuals work at all levels of these worldwide organizations.

Entertainment produced for the masses still dominates entertainment products, from movies to television to music, but the industry is also home to thousands of niche markets. There's a place in this vast multilingual, multicultural arena for virtually anyone who has the stamina and determination to enter this fast-paced industry.

Recorded Music

Record companies, often referred to as "labels," make money by gaining control over a master recording of a performance by an artist and then selling copies to consumers. The acquiring of masters is referred to as the A & R (artist and repertoire) function. The function is easy to explain; the industry itself is more complex. Within individual labels or companies, the jobs are many and varied:

Label president

Business affairs specialist

Legal representative

Bilingual rap artist

Lyricist

Producer

Salesperson

Promoter

Public relations specialist

Artist relations representative

Composer

Musician

Talent agent

Vocalist

Technician

Researcher

Movies

To understand the potential for jobs for foreign language aficionados in the motion picture industry, you have to think of
movies in terms of their economic as well as their artistic function. Movies were once shown exclusively in theaters. Now theater exhibition represents only a small portion of a movie's profit
potential. A hit movie will begin at its first "window"—a movie
theater in the United States or abroad. Then it appears in other
windows of exhibition: video shops, pay-per-view television,
cable television, network television, and syndicated television.
Organizing and supervising this process is the work of thousands
of people.

A critical task of anyone who supervises distribution of a
product is to understand the receptiveness of customers—what
do people want? What moves them, what excites them? At the
front end of the process are the individuals who come up with
ideas for movies that people will enjoy. They write them, script
them, direct them, and produce them. Then there are those who
distribute the movies. In both these areas, cross-cultural and foreign language skills are increasingly sought after.

A career in motion pictures may mean work in any one of a
dozen capacities. Here are a few of your options:

Screenwriter

Director

Animation artist

Producer

Cinematographer

Photographer

On-screen talent

Makeup artist

Stunt performer

Driver

Set designer

Casting director

Reviewer

Subsidiary rights agent

Script adapter

Story analyst

Story editor

Media liaison

Distribution specialist

Creativity, Art, and Design

Do you possess a creative streak? Creative consultant Roger von
Oech wrote about a large company that wanted to develop creativity among its research and design personnel. The company
hired a team of psychologists to discover what made some
employees more creative than others. What they found out was

that the creative people thought they were creative and the less creative people didn't think they were. As a result, said von Oech, people who thought they were creative paid attention to their small ideas, played around with them, and built on them. The "I'm not creative" people were generally too practical in their thinking.

Your mission, should you choose to accept it, is to admit to yourself and then state openly that you are a creative person and then work to prove it. Technology has provided you with unlimited opportunities to develop your creativity and play with your ideas. Add your cross-cultural and language capabilities to a belief in your own creativity, and you could be on the threshold of a great career. According to an essay by Ed Roberts in Alberto Greco's *The Media and Entertainment Industries*, "A computer gives the average person, a high school freshman, the power to do things in a week that all the mathematicians who ever lived until thirty years ago couldn't do." The same could be said of artists, graphic designers, and creative people of all disciplines.

Here are some potential areas where jobs and career opportunities exist for those who admit they're creative:

Animation artist

Comic book writer

Graphic designer

Electronic game designer

Graphic artist

Virtual reality designer

Web page master

Video catalog editor

Cartoonist

CD-ROM editor

Video streaming specialist

Creative consultant

Product Management and Marketing Research

In these days of E-commerce and global markets, it would be difficult to think of any job that is closer to the heart of a company than that of product management and marketing. In the media and entertainment fields, emerging technologies are rapidly transforming the landscape. Multimedia technologies, virtual reality, high definition television, and flat-panel displays have transformed images, sound, and text into nonlinear, interactive communication. The commercial media have moved away from passive content delivery toward targeted message transmissions that solicit consumer responses. Thus, product managers and marketers have to understand the receptiveness of consumers. For this reason, there is an increasing interest in workers who have foreign language skills and who are cross-culturally adept. For careers in this field, computer and statistical capabilities are essential, and research skills are vital. According to experts, problem formulation, data collection, data analysis and interpretation, and communication abilities are skills people use every day in product management and marketing.

CHAPTER NINE

Health Care Careers

ealth care is one of the fastest growing and most
human-resource-intensive industries in the United
States and abroad. There are two broad job categories
in health care: health-diagnosing occupations and health assessment and treating occupations.

Health-diagnosing occupations include these job titles:

Chiropractor

Dentist

Optometrist

Physician

Podiatrist

Health assessment and treating occupations include these
professionals:

Dietitians and nutritionist

Occupational therapist

Pharmacist

Physical therapist

Physician assistant

Recreational therapist

Registered nurse

Respiratory therapist

Speech-language pathologist and audiologist

All told, some 671,000 persons are employed in health diagnosing positions, and more than two million people work in health assessment and treating occupations in this country. (The majority—1,577,000—of this latter category are registered nurses.) Knowledge of other languages is a distinct asset in all of these occupations.

Most health workers deal directly with people, and because increasing numbers of people needing health services in the United States speak something other than English as the primary language, the need for foreign language-capable people in the health professions is high.

There are many medical-related tasks that require people who work behind the scenes using foreign language skills to help people get healthy and stay healthy. Following is a list of jobs and positions in health care:

Dental assistant

Dental hygienist

Eietary aide

Emergency medical technician

Hospital care investigator

Licensed practical nurse

Paramedic

Physician

Registered nurse

Surgeon

Requirements

Before you investigate specific jobs, you should consider your attitude toward the health profession. Would you enjoy working with people who have health or emotional problems? Do you have the type of personality that would make you able to work in an atmosphere where conditions are often hectic and demand a combination of tact and decisiveness?

All of these professions require, of course, special training. The health-diagnosing occupations require doctorates. Four to six years of college—plus many hours of practicum—is generally the minimum level of training required for the health assessment and treating occupations.

There are, however, some health related occupations that require much less training. You may want to work in one of these jobs to get a better sense of health-related work before you invest in the many years of training that many of the health occupations require. Some of these jobs are highlighted next.

Job Descriptions

If you are interested in a health care position, then the next step in your plan is to consider the opportunities that are available for you to use language skills that you have, or that you may develop, in health care jobs. Here is a description of some jobs in the health field that you can consider.

Ambulatory Care Technician

People in hospitals, clinics, and nursing homes who are unable to move around completely on their own require technicians to help. When people can't walk and have trouble making their needs known because of language barriers, their frustration levels rise. Your training in a foreign language, even if it is minimal, could help people both move around and communicate.

Biomedical Equipment Technician

More and more machines and instruments are being developed to test people and assist them with various kinds of ailments. People who operate these biomedical machines must be trained technicians. But they should also be "people" persons because people undergoing medical testing are often nervous and upset. If you can explain biomedical procedures quietly and effectively in the language with which the person is most comfortable, you will help the person, and you will help the whole team that is trying to make that person well.

Mental Health Assistant

The mental health assistant doesn't work with instruments and machines the way the biomedical technician does. But mental health assistants also need specialized training. They need skills in psychology and human behavior. With the increasing stress of modern society, with the high incidence of drug- and alcohol-related illnesses, there is a growing need for mental health assistants. If people have emotional problems and also are unable to communicate to mental health workers because of language difficulties, the situation is obviously very serious. You can use mental health training and your language skills to help such people and perhaps move forward to a very rewarding career in the mental health profession.

Medical Records Clerk

You may be attracted to the health profession, but working directly with people may not be what you do best. That's fine because there are jobs in the health field where you can contribute much without dealing directly with the patients. With the vast number of immigrants, tourists, and foreign visitors to our country, we can expect that there will be health problems. All health problems need to be documented. You may find it rewarding to use your language skills in helping health care professionals translate health documents and health insurance forms into English.

Allied Health Professionals

This group of health care professionals includes respiratory, occupational, and physical therapists; radiology (x-ray) technicians; medical technologists; and phlebotomists (those who draw blood). All of these professions involve patient contact and involve doing medical procedures that can be stressful and painful. Any second language skills will be invaluable in alleviating trauma for the patient. Speaking the patient's native language will enable the health care professional to do a better job, resulting in better medical care.

Patients who are able to communicate with their health care givers and to clearly understand what is being done to them, and why it is being done, are better able to cooperate with the procedure and less anxious about their treatment. As a health care worker, it is also extremely beneficial to be able to explain the procedure to the patient's family or friends. A second language skill that facilitates such communication can greatly ease the anxiety associated with health care.

Licensed Practical Nurse, Nurse's Aide

This group of health care workers has by far the greatest amount of patient contact. Nurses who have language skills that enable them to talk with their patients and receive feedback from patients are able to give the best possible care, with the best possible results.

Nurses also have the most interaction with the patient's family and friends, and clear communication with them can be crucial in establishing a medical history and in relieving anxiety and stress in both the patients and their loved ones. The nurse often serves as a go-between for the patient and the physician. Therefore, the clearer the clinical picture the nurse is able to obtain, the better the treatment the whole health care team can provide.

Emergency Medical Technician

These people respond to all sorts of emergencies. For reasons similar to those listed above, a second language ability that reflects the demographics of the area where they work can be a crucial, perhaps even life-saving, skill for EMTs. Since they must respond to emergency calls, EMTs are not always able to predict the language of the patient. Often the patient is unconscious, and in such cases communication with the family or witnesses of the accident can be vital to the success of treatment. This can be a very stressful occupation but also a very rewarding one that offers an opportunity to use many skills, including second language capabilities.

Some organizations that need people with foreign language skills are CARE, the World Health Organization, Red Cross International, and the American Friends Service Committee.

For More Information

The following organizations should be helpful in gathering further information on health care careers. It is always a good idea to include a self-addressed, stamped envelope with your request.

American Association for Respiratory Care
11030 Ables Lane
Dallas, TX 75229
www..aarc.org

American Association of Colleges of Osteopathic Medicine
   (AACOM)
5550 Friendship Boulevard, Suite 310
Chevy Chase, MD 20815
www.aacom.org

American Dental Education Association (ADEA)
1625 Massachusetts Avenue NW, Suite 600
Washington, DC 20036
www.aads.jhu.edu

American Association of Occupational Therapy
4720 Montgomery Lane
P.O. Box 31220
Bethesda, MD 20824
www.aota.org

American Medical Association (AMA)
515 North State Street
Chicago, IL 60610
www.ama-assn.org

American Nurses Association (ANA)
600 Maryland Avenue SW, Suite 100 W
Washington, DC 20024
www.nursingworld.org

American Optometric Association (AOA)
243 Lindbergh Boulevard
St. Louis, MO 63141
www.aoanet.org

American Physical Therapy Association (APTA)
1111 North Fairfax Street
Alexandria, VA 22314
www.apta.org

American Society of Health-System Pharmacists
7272 Wisconsin Avenue
Bethesda, MD 20814
www.ashp.org

American Speech-Language-Hearing Association (ASHA)
10801 Rockville Pike
Rockville, MD 20852
www.asha.org

American Veterinary Medical Association (AVMA)
1931 North Meacham Road, Suite 100
Schaumburg, IL 60173
www.avma.org

Association of American Medical Colleges
2450 N Street NW
Washington, DC 20037
www.aamc.org

Association of American Veterinary Medical Colleges
   (AAVMC)
1101 Vermont Avenue NW, Suite 710
Washington, DC 20005
www.aavmc.org

Association of Physician Assistant Programs
950 North Washington Street
Alexandria, VA 22314-1552
www.apap.org

Association of Schools and Colleges of Optometry (ASCO)
6110 Executive Boulevard, Suite 510
Rockville, MD 20852
www.opted.org

International Chiropractors Association (ICA)
1110 North Glebe Road, Suite 1000
Arlington, VA 22201
www.chiropractic.org

National League for Nursing
61 Broadway
New York, NY 10006
www.nln.org

National Student Nurses Association (NSNA)
555 West Fifty-seventh Street
New York, NY 10019
www.nsna.org

National Therapeutic Recreation Society
(affiliated with National Recreation and Park Association)
22377 Belmont Ridge Road
Ashburn, VA 20148

Canadian Health Care Organizations

Aboriginal Nurses Association of Canada
12 Stirling Avenue, Third Floor
Ottawa, ON K1Y 1P8
Canada
www.anac.on.ca

Canadian Association of Critical Care Nurses
P.O. Box 25322
London, ON N6C 6B1
Canada
www.caccn.ca

Canadian Dental Association
1815 Alta Vista
Ottawa, ON K2G 3Y6
Canada
www.cda-adc.ca

Canadian Institute for Health Information (CIHI)
377 Dalhousie Street, Suite 200
Ottawa, ON K1N 9N8
Canada
www.cihi.ca

Canadian Nurses Association
50 Driveway
Ottawa, ON K2P 1E2
Canada
www.cna-nurses.ca

Canadian Osteopathic and Medical Association
110-4935 Fortieth Avenue NW
Calgary, AB T3A 2N1
Canada
www.ccmadoctors.ca

Canadian Physiotherapy Association
2345 Yonge Street, Suite 410
Toronto, ON M4P 2E5
Canada
www.physiotherapy.ca0

CHAPTER TEN

Travel and Tourism

The travel industry has grown beyond the Department of Labor's expectations since the first edition of this book, and so has the need for multilingual employees in travel, transportation, and tourism. If your second language is Chinese, you could find yourself planning panda-watching trips starting in Chengdu or plotting voyages to Tibet. But you don't have to be a Chinese speaker to wind up planning exotic excursions. Nowadays, virtually any language will do.

Whether it is for business or pleasure, travelers today expect more for their money, and that includes being able to communicate with travel representatives in airports, on cruise ships, or on the Orient Express. All of the associated businesses—such as car rentals, skycaps, luggage handlers, reservation and ticket clerks, hotel reservations, and convention planners—are looking for employees who speak more than one language. They must be able to provide services for customers from all over the world.

About half of the country's travel agents work in suburban areas and make up a large portion of the travel industry's personnel. They may still be considered the backbone of the industry even though they are being challenged by the advances in technology that allow travelers to make their own travel plans and to buy their tickets on the Internet.

Agents are more specialized in today's fast-paced world of travel. International agents must provide information on customs regulations, passports, visas, vaccination certificates, and other health-related requirements. Their customers want the latest information on current exchange rates and travel tips of all kinds.

The travel agent's workload varies, depending on the season and the economy. Travel into the United States is influenced by the strength of the dollar and other factors. Naturally, more tourists visit the United States when the exchange rate is favorable to foreign currencies. Special events such as the Olympics or other international events attract visitors. Sophisticated marketing of travel opportunities also has an effect.

Even though tourism and foreign travel continue to grow in the United States, the common problem of poor communication remains a barrier in many areas of the travel industry. International travel agents indicated in a survey that language is one of the most serious problems in attracting foreign travelers to the United States. Former senator Paul Simon once noted that the Immigration and Naturalization Service should erect a sign at our international airports: "Welcome to the United States. We do not speak your language."

Progress has been made in the last twenty years. The United States has many more language-qualified people in the travel and tourism industry than there were in the 1970s and 1980s. But there are still not enough to serve the vast numbers of foreign visitors who arrive each year. The travel and tourism industry needs language-qualified employees at all levels.

In terms of job prospects for people with the ability to speak more than one language, the potential is great. If you work for a travel agency, you can certainly help your U.S. clients more effectively if you are able to talk to people abroad in the language of their countries, or at least in a language other than English.

Working Conditions and Skills Required

Travel agents spend most of their time working behind a desk—conferring with clients, punching alternate schedules into a computer in a search for the best rates and connections, making car rental and hotel reservations, and arranging for group travel. During peak travel times, agents typically are under a great deal of pressure, and, especially if they own their own businesses, they often work long hours. Pay for beginners is modest. Managers earn better salaries. The travel industry is sensitive to economic recessions, when people tend to put off their travel plans.

Travel agents need good interpersonal skills. You need to be a good salesperson—pleasant, patient, and able to gain the confidence of your clients.

The same skills are required for personnel in the airline industry and the hotel and resort business. *Travel Weekly* listed the world's top ten tourism destinations as France, Spain, the United States, Italy, China, the United Kingdom, Canada, Mexico, the Russian Federation, and Poland. Because Americans are not known for their language skills, it stands to reason that an increasing number of multilingual tour guides and travel employees are needed as travelers flock to the popular tourist destinations. Language problems often aggravate ordinary day-to-day problems. One visitor complained that he was unable to find tasty and nutritious vegetarian meals in those parts of the United States in which he wanted to travel. No one had thought of providing a list of vegetarian eating places where Hindu visitors could eat without violating their religious beliefs.

Training

Nobody is excited by the prospect of hiring an inexperienced travel agent, so how do you get trained? There are several options.

Many private vocational schools offer full-time programs lasting from three to twelve weeks. Some schools offer weekend and/or evening courses. There are even some colleges that offer a bachelor's or master's degree in travel and tourism.

You may want to check out such places as Florida International University School of Hospitality Management if you are looking for training that will lead to a job in the tourism and travel industry. Cornell University in the state of New York prides itself on its prestigious and well-respected School of Hotel Administration. The program presents a strong business curriculum focused on the hospitality industry. The Statler Hotel, located on the campus, is a full-service hotel and executive facility managed and staffed by the students of the School of Hotel Administration.

The University of Nevada, Las Vegas, is renowned for its William F. Harrah College of Hotel Administration as well as a department of tourism and convention administration. This university is committed to providing cutting-edge educational opportunities in a range of tourism and hospitality fields, including casinos, clubs, conventions and expositions, entertainment food services, and lodging and resort industries. It is clear that the travel, transportation, and tourism industry has grown far beyond the individual travel agent. It's a big business world in its own right. If you speak more than one language, you may have an exciting career ahead.

Courses in foreign languages, geography, history, and computer use are useful for aspiring travel agents. If you want to start your own agency (you should be an experienced travel agent first), courses in accounting and business management also are helpful. Agencies like their employees to have a college degree (in anything), although this is often stated as a preference rather than a requirement.

In addition to courses offered by colleges and vocational schools, training is available from travel associations. The American Society of Travel Agents (ASTA) and the Institute of Certified Travel Agents offer a correspondence course. Once you become an experienced travel agent, you may want to take an advanced, eighteen-month, part-time course offered by the Institute of Certified Travel Agents. This gives you the title of

Certified Travel Counselor. Another recognized mark of achievement is the certificate of proficiency offered by the American Society of Travel Agents to those who pass the three-hour examination.

Whatever course of study you choose, education is an important part of preparing to become part of the travel industry. Two other factors are also key to your success: work experience and travel. On-the-job training is invaluable. You may want to start by taking some courses and then applying for part-time work as an airline reservations clerk or receptionist in the travel industry. With experience and education, you will advance. If you can afford it, travel is another way to make yourself ready for a career in the travel industry. Firsthand experience of vacation spots allows you to better inform clients about what awaits them when they leave for their trips.

The tremendous impact of computer technology on the workplace finds us booking our own travel schedules and buying tickets on the Internet. Students and job seekers alike can make this technology work for them by finding a job on one of the many websites employers use to find qualified employees. We recently accessed the Workplace Channel and found more than fifty jobs posted for travel agents at all levels of expertise. Take your language skills, get out there, and find a job!

Related Job Opportunities

Airport Personnel

Working at an airport can give you an opportunity to practice your language and service skills. Everyone from bus drivers and skycaps to food service and security personnel may well be in frequent daily contact with people who don't speak English and who need assistance or service. If you have people skills and some level of language capability, you can launch a career in tourism and travel by working at an airport.

Other opportunities to use foreign language skills come from working directly for the airlines. Pilots and flight attendants assigned to international routes have an obvious chance to speak a language other than English on the job. It takes time and training to be assigned to these positions of responsibility, but the work is well worth considering if you have language skills and an interest in flying. And although language skills are not required for these jobs, knowing another language does give job candidates an edge in a tough market. It also makes assignment to international flights more likely once you have secured a job with the airlines.

Hotels and Motels

Some large metropolitan hotels have employees who are fluent in as many as five different languages. These individuals serve as desk clerks, cashiers, front office personnel, and in other positions. As travel tourism increases in the United States, the need for bilingual or multilingual personnel in the hospitality industry—hotels, motels, restaurants—has expanded from the elite metropolitan establishments to the small hotels, inns, and motels in towns and cities across America. The way foreign visitors are turning up in places like Lawrence, Kansas, and Pensacola, Florida, it is clear that English-only hotel and motel workers will be underprepared to serve future guests.

For More Information

For details on travel careers, contact the following professional associations:

American Society of Travel Agents (ASTA)
1101 King Street, Suite 200
Alexandria, VA 22314
www.astanet.com

Air Line Pilots Association International
P.O. Box 1169
Herndon, VA 20172
www.alpa.org

Association of Flight Attendants
1275 K Street NW, Suite 580
Washington, DC 20036
www.flightattendant-afa.org

Institute of Certified Travel Agents
148 Linden Street
P.O. Box 812059
Wellesley, MA 02482
www.icta.com

Florida International University
School of Hospitality Management
3000 Northeast 151st Street, HM 210
North Miami, FL 33181
www.fiu.edu/~hospman

School of Hotel Administration
Cornell University
Ithaca, NY 14853
www.hotelschool.cornell.edu

College of Hotel Administration
University of Nevada Las Vegas
4505 Maryland Parkway
Box 456013
Las Vegas, NV 89154
www.unlv.edu/Colleges/Hotel

Canadian Travel and Hospitality Programs

Hotel-Motel Administration

Northern Alberta Institute of Technology
11762 - 106th Street NW
Edmonton, AB T5G 3H1
Canada

Southern Alberta Institute of Technology
1301 Sixteenth Avenue NW
Calgary, AB T2M 0L4
Canada

British Columbia Institute of Technology
37 Wilingdon Avenue
Burnaby, BC V5G 3H2
Canada

Camosun College
Landsdowne Campus
3100 Foul Bay Road
Victoria, BC V8P 5J5
Canada

Malasprina College
900 Fifth Street
Nanaimo, BC V9R 5S5
Canada

Tourism and Travel Management

Grant MacEwan Community College
10700 - 104th Avenue
Edmonton, AB T5J 4S2
Canada

British Columbia Institute of Technology
3700 Wilingdon Avenue
Burnaby, BC V5G 3H2
Canada

Algonquin College of Applied Arts and Technology
1385 Woodroffe Avenue
Nepean, ON K2G 1V8
Canada

Fanshawe College
1460 Oxford Street East
P.O. Box 7005
London, ON N5Y 5R6
Canada

Ryerson Polytechnic Institute
350 Victoria Street
Toronto, ON M5B 2K3
Canada

CHAPTER ELEVEN

Local and Federal Government

V irtually all the jobs described so far can be found in one form or another within the programs of the federal government: social sciences, librarianship, protection, translation, health care, and more. If you pursue any of these jobs within the federal system, most of what has already been discussed will still apply. The U.S. and Canadian governments maintain job search websites on the Internet. Some of the most useful are listed at the end of the chapter. In addition, there are unique requirements and responsibilities involved with working for the government.

The federal government represents the biggest bureaucracy in the nation. You must be a team worker and be able to deal with the red tape and intricacies of this huge enterprise. Some people enjoy the connections and interplay and other challenges involved with a huge, complex system. If you are one of these people, government jobs can be very satisfying, and there are many varied opportunities for multilingual work.

Opportunities and Rewards

Working for the federal government is different from working anywhere else. If you are unsure about getting into government work, internships provide a good way to explore the option. Many branches of the federal government offer both paid and unpaid internships that will give you good firsthand knowledge of both multilingual and government work. Whether you choose to continue with a government career or decide it is not for you, the experience will prove very valuable in improving your language and job skills.

Employment opportunities within the federal government are greater and more far-ranging and varied than most people realize. One of the most difficult parts of getting a job with the government is finding out about openings. One of the best ways to do this is to apply for job information from the specific department in which you wish to work.

The pay and advancement for all civil service jobs is very rigid and set by the very strict, structured guidelines of the GS system. Most language related jobs will fall in the GS-5 to GS-11 range.

There is a category of "excepted" jobs. Employees in excepted service jobs receive similar pay but are not subject to the same exam and testing procedures nor are they affected by other GS guidelines such as extra points for veteran status.

Excepted jobs are sometimes offered on limited contracts and sometimes last only for a finite contract period. Benefits such as retirement, saving plans, insurance, and leave are very good for civil service jobs and often these are extended to excepted service employees.

With government jobs, there are requirements you won't often find if you apply for work elsewhere. Government jobs often require you to be fingerprinted. When some level of security clearance is necessary, details of your past may be investigated, and you may be required to take a polygraph test.

Many of the language-related jobs will require travel, and that can be a disadvantage or an advantage depending on your point of view. Working in the government may also restrict your involvement with various political parties to avoid conflicts of interest.

Language Proficiency

Language proficiency to qualify for a job is based heavily on tests. Most departments rely on the Foreign Service Institute or Inter-Agency Language Round Table proficiency ratings, which rate prospective employees from 0 to 5 according to the results of the testing. As we all know, written structured testing is not always the most accurate way of judging language and communication skills. And if your on-the-job performance does not match the level estimated by the test, you will be let go.

The U.S. Department of State has many jobs that require foreign language proficiency (usually at a 3+ rating on a 5-point rating scale). The most common State Department programs that do are:

Foreign Service

Human Rights and Humanitarian Affairs

Bureau of Intelligence and Research

Refugee Programs

The Agency for International Development is one of several other divisions attached to the State Department that also seek employees with foreign language skills. There are also language-related positions in other government agencies, including the Department of Defense, the National Security Agency, the Central Intelligence Agency, and the Immigration and Naturalization Service.

The particular languages most in demand depend on the political circumstances of the day. At this writing, the languages most in demand are Arabic (and dialects), Chinese (and dialects), Russian, Korean, Japanese, Farsi, and Polish.

In addition to language skills, prospective government employees should have an interest in other cultures and in living abroad. They should be able to adapt quickly to the country where they are assigned. Sometimes this means adjustments in lifestyle. For example, Anthony, an employee of the Agency for International Development, was stationed in Afghanistan. He reports that one of the strains of living in Muslim countries is that it is considered gross by most local people to show any affection in public toward your wife. Hand holding and good-bye kisses are to be avoided. Even in the privacy of your home, you must exercise discretion because the servants may be offended and report the offensive behavior to their friends and associates. Even so, Anthony was willing to adjust, and he enjoyed many fruitful years living in various Muslim countries.

For More Information

For more detailed information on jobs with the federal government, write to:

U.S. Department of State
Bureau of Personnel
Office of Recruitment, Examination, and Employment
Washington, DC 20520

Law Enforcement, Corrections, and Fire Fighting

Police officers and related personnel, corrections officers, and firefighters render vital services to any community, and persons in these occupations are generally highly respected. There are, of course, dangers associated with these jobs, and they should be given serious consideration when you are contemplating a job in protective services or corrections.

These jobs can be dangerous and stressful for both those working in the field and for their families. You need to consider that your work will bring you into contact with many of the most unpleasant aspects of our society, and it takes a toughness to face the work day after day. At the same time, your direct service to people of your community offers many satisfactions. Your contributions to your community and to society are concrete, and many find great satisfaction in these jobs.

Requirements and Training

For all of the jobs described above, it is necessary to have a high school diploma or the equivalent. You must also be a U.S. citizen. Training beyond high school is also required, and the length and type of training will depend on the job you are seeking. Many universities and community colleges offer one-and two-year programs in law enforcement and related fields, and police, fire, and correction departments offer training academies. The need for bilingual and multilingual skills in these occupations is very apparent, especially in large metropolitan areas. Workers need to first have good written and verbal communication skills in English. Gathering data, interviewing witnesses, record keeping, taking notes, and writing clear concise reports are important parts of all these occupations.

Many of the people encountered daily in large cities will not speak English as the primary language, and some will not speak it at all. For law enforcement personnel, being able to communicate with these people in their primary languages has many advantages. And possessing the language skills necessary to do so will make you very valuable and improve your performance and safety on the job. Your language skills need to be such that people speaking with you will be confident that they are being understood, and you must be sure you are understood by them as well. Here schoolbook perfection is not required; it's knowing the language of the street and the expressions of the specific subcultures with which you will be dealing that is important.

Employers are especially seeking people from the minority groups that they will serve. In times of stress and danger, language can be the difference between life and death, and the benefits are enhanced when the officer or firefighter not only speaks the language but is identifiable as a member of the community ethnic group. Current literature and projections for the future specifically mention a great need for Hispanic and Chinese language proficiencies and backgrounds in these professions.

Police Enforcement

Police officers are increasingly required to exhibit social and cultural sensitivity. If you have an interest in law enforcement at the local, state, or national level, your efforts will be enhanced by language and cultural skills. Even in small communities in rural settings, police and sheriff's department personnel are being hired because of their skills in a second language. At the state level, the highway patrol and state investigative agencies are seeking officers and detectives with language skills. The FBI and other federal government law enforcement organizations all have policies that call for increased numbers of second-language qualified personnel.

A riot erupted in Washington, D.C., when an English-speaking police officer arrested an inebriated Spanish-speaking man one weekend in a park in the Hispanic area of the city. The arrested man and his friends didn't see anything wrong with getting drunk in the park on a Sunday afternoon. Several million dollars of property damage resulted, and a curfew was in effect for a week. Tensions had built up in the Hispanic community over what they regarded as heavy-handed police tactics. Significantly, of the five thousand or so police officers in the District, fewer than a hundred spoke Spanish at the time, and few of these were stationed in the Spanish-speaking parts of the city. Hiring officers with second-language skills can be a very cost-effective move and a good way to help improve the relationship between the police and the community in tense times.

Corrections

People who work in the protective services and correctional centers should have a strong sense of social justice and responsibility. Corrections officers work with people who have broken the law or have had some other brush with the legal system. Here the need is for people who can explain laws and legal terms to persons whose primary language is not English. As social diversity continues to increase, more people with second-language skills are needed in law enforcement and corrections positions.

Firefighters

Like law enforcement personnel, firefighters are found in all communities and are responsible to protect all segments of the community. In big cities where there are large foreign language communities concentrated in certain areas, it may be a matter of life or death for firefighters to be able to understand victims of fires or explosions who are trying to tell them about friends and loved ones who are trapped or in danger.

There was a fire in an apartment building in Washington, D.C. Most of the building's inhabitants were Spanish-speaking people from Central America. None of the firefighters on the scene spoke Spanish, so their instructions to the building's inhabitants were not understood. In this job, a lack of communication can be life threatening.

For More Information

United States

The U.S. Government's official website for jobs and employment information is provided by the U.S. Office of Personnel Management at www.usajobs.opm.gov.

Canada

The Canadian government's employment programs can be found at www.canada.gc.ca/programs/jobs_e.html.

Indian and Northern Affairs Canada
www.inac.gc.ca/ai/aw/nlcts_e.html (for a complete list of
    national contacts and opportunities for Aboriginal students)

Services Branch of Public Works and Government
    Services for Canada
www.canada.gc.ca/programs/jobs

Public Service Commission of Canada
www.psc-cfp.gc.ca/jobs.htm
(Manages the hiring process for the federal civil
    service in Canada)

Canadian Internships
www.campusaccess.com
(Database of internships and volunteer organizations)

Federal Public Sector Youth Internship Program
www.inac.gc.ca/ai/aw/ase_e.html

CHAPTER TWELVE

Language-Intensive Jobs: Translating, Interpreting, Teaching

T ranslating, interpreting, and teaching are jobs people tend to think of first when seeking ways to use their foreign language skills. These occupations all require exceptional written and oral fluency in the target language.

Translating and Interpreting

Translators and interpreters transfer information from one language to another. Translators work with written information, and interpreters with spoken information. Both try to achieve a minimum of distortion in the process. Not only should the message of the translation or interpretation be the same as the original, but the style and emotional content of the statement should be comparable to the original. A good translator or interpreter does not impose his or her own style, interpretation, or opinion onto the translation or interpretation.

But just because a person is bilingual does not mean that he or she will be a good translator or, especially, a good interpreter. Some people have a special gift for this work, and even they must train and practice to be effective.

There are about ten thousand translators and interpreters working in the United States, many working only part-time. The market tendency seems to favor interpreters over translators. In the State Department, for example, contract interpreters number around twelve hundred, while contract translators number around two hundred.

Both translators and interpreters require the highest level of second-language skills. Translators almost always translate from the second language into their native language, but this is not always the case with interpreters. Both of these occupations require extensive knowledge of the native language as well as the second language and require, as well, a sound understanding of the culture or cultures associated with the target language.

Translators must be meticulous students of language patterns, grammar, and idiomatic meaning. Persons interested in interpretation should be good with people, be good listeners, and have clear speech. Both translators and interpreters will be in greater demand and have more interesting jobs if they are interested in a wide range of subjects and are knowledgeable in a variety of areas. Some interpreters work in the court systems, usually on a freelance basis, interpreting the depositions of witnesses who do not speak English and providing interpretation for the defendants.

Neyde supplements her income as a college teacher by on-call interpreting for the local courts during her vacations. She finds this freelance interpreting (in Portuguese, Spanish, French, and Italian) challenging and interesting. One thing to note is that the hourly pay differs according to the language. For example, Neyde is paid more than twice the amount for Portuguese as for Spanish. To get these jobs, she registered with different agencies, such as the Immigration and Naturalization Service.

An important skill for interpreters and translators is to know the various resources available to find information. Research is an important part of this job. If you are interested in lots of things, have excellent primary and secondary language skills, and like meeting new people or writing, this might be the career for you.

Employers

The federal government is the largest single employer of translators and interpreters. These federal agencies include the State Department, FBI, National Security Agency, Central Intelligence Agency, Agency for International Development, Library of Congress, U.S. District Courts, and the U.S. Information Agency. Other employers include the United Nations, international agencies such as the International Development Bank, the Telecommunications Satellite Organization, the Organization of American States, the Pan-American Health Organization, and some private industries. Frequently, translators will be self-employed, people who are contracted by companies to translate a personnel manual or a piece of business correspondence. Large international companies such as IBM have full-time translators on board. Guadalupe, an English-Spanish-Portuguese translator working for an international electronic firm, specializes in technical documents and has a team of translators working for her. Translators and interpreters will have more job opportunities if they know several languages.

Most American service organizations and businesses do not employ translators, but their translations are provided by employees whose primary job is not language related. These employers consider a second language a very valuable secondary skill.

Freelance translators are generally paid by the number of words (or pages), either in the original or the translation. Rates vary from $20 to $100 per thousand words. A good freelance translator can earn a decent living and enjoy the benefit of a flexible work schedule. Freelance interpreters who are certified U.S. District or Circuit Court interpreters currently earn $165 for a half day or $305 for a full day.

Job Requirements

The same high-level language skills required by translation are also needed to work as an interpreter, with the added necessity of a fluency with the spoken word. Nuance and accent can be very important in oral communication. Employers of interpreters are usually high government or business officials. Therefore, an understanding of protocol, customs, and etiquette is essential for interpreters who wish to efficiently and unobtrusively facilitate conversation between the parties they are interpreting for.

Those interested in careers in this area need more than a knowledge of a second language. Translators and interpreters alike should read widely in the language they will be translating. Newspapers, magazines, catalogs, and general materials of all sorts are helpful. Travel in countries where the language is spoken is invaluable, especially for the interpreter. Most interpreters have spoken several languages all of their lives. United Nations interpreters need native or near-native fluency in at least three of the six official languages of the United Nations: Arabic, Chinese, English, French, Russian, and Spanish. These positions are very competitive.

The translator may hone his or her skills through courses in journalism and technical writing. Familiarity with the jargon of many fields will greatly enhance the value of a translator or interpreter. There are special translator/interpreter training programs at some universities. Russian, German, Japanese, French, and Spanish are the languages most in demand. There is a growing need for interpreters and translators in Portuguese, Chinese, and Arabic. A couple of broad areas of knowledge (math, science, business) as well as extensive language skills will enable the interpreter or translator to have the greatest number of career options.

Foreign Language Teaching

We are all familiar with foreign language teaching; most of us have enrolled in foreign language classes. Many of you may have been inspired to use your second language by one of the fifty thousand grade school, high school, or college foreign language teachers. In the current job market, these teaching jobs are quite competitive. On the primary or secondary school level, they require a bachelor's degree, and often a master's degree, plus teacher certification, which often involves one or two years of education courses.

About 20 percent of elementary schools and 90 percent of secondary schools offer foreign language instruction. Most of these jobs are for Spanish, French, German, and Latin, in descending order of popularity. Career opportunities on the college level are scarce because most students are taught by graduate assistants, especially at the larger universities.

Bilingual Education Programs

Currently, it is easier to find jobs in bilingual education than it is in foreign language teaching. Bilingual programs are for students from non-English-speaking homes who will profit from having subject matter taught in a language they can understand. Bilingual teachers, most of whom are employed on the primary school level, may teach science, math, social studies, or language arts— in the students' native language.

Employers (school superintendents and principals) look for people who are fluent in the requisite language. This is usually Spanish in the United States, but on occasion may be any one of a hundred other languages. Prospective bilingual teachers need to have a college degree (or two) and be interested in taking the education courses needed to gain state certification if they do not already possess it. If you are interested in teaching in a bilingual program, and there is a Hispanic or other ethnic community in your area whose language and culture you know, call the local school superintendent to find out the prospects. A related field, teaching English as a second language, was the subject of Chapter 3.

Anthropology

There are other teachers who often find fluency in a second language to be especially useful. Anthropologists and political scientists are two examples.

Anthropologists study the origins, cultures, traditions, beliefs, politics, and social relationships of the world's people. They often live abroad for extended periods, and they may hold teaching positions in universities or colleges. A Ph.D. is generally required for teaching at the university level.

Political Science

Political scientists study government at all levels, from the smallest native village to the international community of nations. Foreign language skills are important not only to those who are concerned with international relations and foreign political systems but also to those interested in the dynamics of local politics.

Cross-cultural and ethnic/linguistic interaction plays an important part in local elections, community development plans, and community solidarity efforts. If you have special interest in politics, the development of your language and cultural skills can help move your career plans forward.

For More Information

American Association of Language Specialists
1000 Connecticut Avenue NW, Suite 9
Washington, DC 20036
www.taals.net

American Council on the Teaching of Foreign Languages
6 Executive Plaza
Yonkers, NY 10701
www.actfl.org

American Literary Translators Association
Box 830688, MC35
University of Texas
Richardson, TX 75083
www.utdallas.edu

American Translators Association (ATA)
225 Reinekers Lane, Suite 590
Alexandria, VA 22314
www.atanet.org

Society of Federal Linguists (SFL)
P.O. Box 7765
Washington, DC 20044
www.federal-linguists.org

National Clearinghouse for Bilingual Education
The George Washington University
Center for the Study of Language and Education
2121 K Street NW, Suite 260
Washington, DC 20037
www.ncbe.gwu.edu

National Association for Bilingual Education (NABE)
1220 L Street NW, Suite 605
Washington, DC 20005
www.nabe.org

Canadian Translators and Interpreters Council (CTIC)
1 Nicholas Street, Suite 1202
Ottawa, ON K1N 7B7
Canada
www.synapse.net/~ctic

CHAPTER THIRTEEN

Consulting

*I*f you have some particular expertise that is in demand internationally, you may want to explore employment as an international consultant. You should possess a graduate degree related to your specialization and speak the language of the country that needs your expertise.

What kinds of expertise are in demand? Rural health care, including nutrition and family planning; rural educational development, mostly at the primary school level but including adult literacy; agriculture, including irrigation techniques; community development; civil engineering; and management, including computer science and accounting, are all areas in which experienced consultants are needed.

Government priorities change at about the same rate as fashions. For example, small business and nonprofit group specialists became priorities for the Agency for International Development in the late 1980s. That has shifted, although not completely. While there is still some demand, no one can predict for certain if a particular specialization will be in demand in the coming decades.

Requirements

How experienced do you have to be? Usually about ten years of experience is needed to be competitive as a consultant. Previous work in the host country is highly desirable, although not normally expected. Familiarity with and an understanding of the host country's culture, infrastructure (both physical and political), and other pertinent facts would considerably enhance your chances.

What's this about advanced degrees? To be competitive for most of these opportunities, you must not only be able to do the job, you must be able to convince a stranger reading your curriculum vitae (a long, more academic type of resume) that your education and training equip you to do the job. In other words, you have to inspire confidence on paper. A master's degree is generally the lowest level of academic preparation sought; a Ph.D. is better. Either of these academic levels added to several years of experience in or familiarity with the area, region, or country would set off green lights for the person or persons reviewing your resume.

What languages are generally required? For much of Africa, English and French are all that most agencies can realistically require. Fluency in particular African languages, of which there are hundreds, would be an asset for community development work where those languages are spoken, but this is rarely required.

One of the authors was attending an international conference in Kinshasa, Zaire. The author, along with two African colleagues, each from a different country, needed to make some logistical arrangements with two young men who were assigned this type of duty. One African colleague began, *"Bwana,"* in Swahili, a common East African lingua franca. The two men did not understand. The colleague then began in another language. They didn't understand this either. He then tried two other African languages. Same result. Then the other colleague tried five languages that he spoke. Same result. At that point, the Swahili-speaking colleague made an unmistakable gesture meaning, "Well, what can you speak?" The two men drew themselves up with some pride, and each counted off on his fingers five or six languages. Among the three of us trying to communicate with our guide/assistants, more than thirteen languages were spoken, but not one language in common.

Spanish is a requirement for much of Latin America, Portuguese for Brazil. Occasionally, and depending on how deeply into the interior of the country you may need to go, a native South American Indian language may be useful. Consultants fluent in an Asian language have a distinct advantage in landing assignments in that area.

Opportunities and Rewards

Who hires international consultants? A lot of companies, apparently. When the authors typed the words "training for international consulting" into a search engine, the Internet came up with more than a half million entries. A number of international companies are listed, with their websites, in Appendix B.

From this list, you can earmark some companies that from time to time may be in need of someone with your special skills. To determine what other companies on the list do, call up their websites on the Internet or look them up in the reference section of your local library. Some of these companies may not be doing as much international business now as they were a few years ago, and others might have changed focus.

Many international companies keep a bank of resumes on hand, unlike most domestic companies, and they will welcome receiving yours. But having your resume on hand does not mean they will actively pursue you. You will have to follow up if an interview is arranged. Don't assume you are in their line of sight. Check back periodically and hammer home your availability.

A typical short-term assignment overseas as a consultant may involve working closely with several people from the funding agency and the national host on a four- to six-week project. The contracts often stipulate a long list of tasks that must be completed. The hours are long; the real workweek is often seven days. Your task may be to figure out how to get the project's objectives accomplished without rubbing people the wrong way. Sometimes a fifty- to one hundred-page report must be written for and approved by the funding source.

Most government agencies or multinational corporations that hire consultants usually have preset compensation scales but occasionally defer to your level of compensation if you are employed full-time and take an assignment on a special basis. When that is the case, some agencies, USAID for example, may calculate your daily wage by dividing your annual income by 260 workdays in a year. If you can document annual income from your job and/or other consulting contracts of say, $40,000, your authorized daily rate would be approximately $154. There are rarely any fringe benefits other than a per diem, which may differ according to living costs in the host country.

How do you land a consulting contract? The majority of the consulting contracts are let to large companies. Funding agencies find their consultants by looking through their banks of resumes or curricula vitae and by calling contacts who suggest names to them. You must sell yourself to the company, which will then submit your curriculum vitae to the funding agency, usually with the CVs of two or three other qualified people. The funding agency will select the consultant it wants from among the two to four CVs. Some longer-term contracts also may be let for periods of one to five years. The compensation package generally is good, and there are generous housing allowances.

Starting Your Own Consulting Business

Unless you are well known and/or well connected, starting your own business is a hard route to go. Most agencies, in spite of professed interest in small companies, want to contract with large companies or universities. Take the example of Mark, who freelanced for many years. While working through established firms, he received many contracts from several government agencies as a short-term consultant abroad. However, when he started his own international consulting firm, those same agencies would not give his company any contracts. Mark complained to the small business advocacy departments within these agencies and was told that "Yes, we encourage small companies to solicit projects. But your company is a start-up company." Another company with revenues of about $2 million a year was told by another government agency to go in with another, bigger company because the agency didn't want to deal with such a small business. Y4our best bet is to get your contracts through an established company.

For more information on careers in international consulting, see Appendix B.

CHAPTER FOURTEEN

Refining Your Job-Search Strategy

C areer specialists generally agree on job-search strategies, which we have refined to incorporate seven simple steps. They involve:

1. Looking within yourself

2. Researching your career field

3. Getting out a resume

4. Networking to refine your job search

5. Obtaining informational (not job) interviews

6. Interviewing for a job

7. Negotiating a job package that suits you

Looking Within

Before you start your job search, you should think about your long-term career aspirations, according to Stephanie Lowell, who wrote a career guide for Harvard Business School. You should write down the experiences you've had and the skills you've developed. What organizational characteristics do you like and dislike (such as size and location)? What do you really care about? What would you enjoy enough to do every day?

Researching Your Career Field

What kind of job are you looking for? There are dozens of Internet websites where you can gauge your skills, post your resume, and browse job listings. Let's say that you're interested in international organizations. There are five kinds:

1. Public multinational (the United Nations, the World Bank, the International Monetary Fund, the Organization of American States, the European Common Market, the North Atlantic Treaty Organization, the Organization for Economic Cooperation and Development)

2. Government (Department of State, Department of Defense, U.S. military forces, Agency for International Development, Department of Agriculture, Central Intelligence Agency, National Security Agency, Peace Corps)

3. Business (banks, Internet companies, manufacturing companies, consulting firms)

4. Educational (American Field Service, Council on International Educational Exchange, Institute on International Education, foundations, universities)

5. Private voluntary (Partners of the Americas, CARE, Save the Children, Foster Parents Plan, the Salvation Army, the Red Cross, the YMCA International Division)

It's important to understand the kind of employee each type of organization seeks. For example, unless you have years of relevant experience and prestigious university degrees, high level jobs at public multinationals are difficult to get. Some government agencies are extremely competitive also. For example, the State Department requires all applicants to pass rigid written and oral examinations. Educational and private voluntary organizations often require special contracts to smooth the way to an international job.

Developing a Resume or Website

The purpose of a resume is not to get the job, it is to get an *interview* that may lead to a job. And when you go to the interview, you want to take another copy of your resume with you. Going to an interview without a resume in your pocket is a big mistake.

What is the best way to create a resume? First, it is crucial to know your own qualifications. Do you have the background and skills that are valued by the people who will hire you in your international job? If so, you will want to highlight these skills in your resume.

Next, it's important to have a career objective. Many resumes state a career objective at the beginning. Often the best place for a specific objective is in a cover letter rather than in the resume. (You don't want to limit your options, do you?) Still, it is a good idea to include a general career objective on your resume that is specific enough to show that you have a definite goal. Then you can state a more specific objective in each cover letter.

There are two general formats for resumes: chronological and functional. A chronological sequence is probably best for most young college graduates, or if you have followed a steady career progression in the same or related fields. If you have been out of the workforce for some time, if your career has had long interruptions, or if you are making a drastic change in careers, then the functional format may be best for you. In this format you focus on achievements and skills. If you are in doubt of which format to use, use the chronological format. It is more conservative, and the people who do the hiring tend to be conservative themselves.

Once you have reviewed your qualifications, formulated an objective, and selected a resume format, it's time to focus on language. Clear, concise, and active are the key concepts here. You want to sound professional, intelligent, and warm. It is so easy to fall into boring prose and irritating jargon that it will be worth your while to pick up a manual or two on writing resumes. (See the bibliography at the end of this chapter.) There are a number of helpful software programs to enable you to turn out a professional-looking resume on a personal computer. Whatever you do, don't misspell any words, and don't lie about your work or educational background.

While you must be honest, you do want to play up your strengths. Describe what skills and accomplishments you had in your jobs (if they are relevant to the kind of job you are trying to get). American executives love "hard numbers." Quantify anything that you can: You were one of two secretaries in a department of eight professional epidemiologists, handling an average of 86 pieces of correspondence and 120 requests for information weekly over a computer network linking 843 health centers specializing in fourteen contagious diseases. You get the point.

And it is equally important to disguise your weaknesses. Some things that are generally considered weaknesses include staying less than three years in a job and being between jobs for more than a few months at a time. These can be finessed by omitting some jobs you were in for only a short time and by rounding off dates to just the year.

If you studied or travelled between jobs, be sure to make that clear. If you did volunteer work, by all means list it. Unpaid experience should be described in the same ways that you describe paid job experience. And don't forget to quantify.

You will want to include a section on education in your resume. If you are straight out of school or if you have a doctorate, list the education section first. If not, list it after the section on professional experience. If you have a college degree, omit reference to your high school experience (unless you were the vale-dictorian). List your college grade point average only if it was quite high. Don't list extracurricular activities unless they have a direct bearing on the job you are trying to get. If you attended college for less than one year, then list the relevant courses.

Be very selective about the "optional" information you include on your resume. By all means include any special skills (comput-er skills, foreign languages) or professional awards. But think twice before you list anything that will turn off a conservative employer. Avoid controversy if you can. If your volunteer experi-ence is with political or social groups that may be seen as con-troversial, you might want to generalize. You could mention that you were involved in civic affairs and community-development projects without naming names. Better still, exclude these items unless they are directly relevant to the job you are seeking.

Finally, you will want to make your resume easy to read. Keep it brief—one or two pages if you possibly can. Prospective employers tend to read only one page. Use white or beige paper (use twenty- or twenty-four-pound paper) and black ink. Provide white space (margins). And use a standard type style (not script or Old English).

If you conduct your job search on-line, be sure that you include key words—industry terms, company names, years of experience, degrees—in your resume. Computer search engines don't read cover letters. Your electronic resume should do both jobs.

Cover Letters

Always send a one-page, single-spaced cover letter with your resume. The letter should state your case, explaining what job you want and why.

Make the letter look great. It should be neat and concise, with no spelling or grammar errors. Use plain paper; no letterheads unless you own the company. Address the letter to a specific person, not to a job title. If you don't know the person's name and title, call the company's switchboard and ask the receptionist.

Like the resume, the cover letter should be brief, usually three paragraphs. In the first, catch the reader's attention: "Your advertisement in the *Wall Street Journal* caught my eye." Mention your objective in the first paragraph. In the second paragraph, sell your accomplishments. Quantify where you can. In the final paragraph, be specific about your plans to contact the organization after the reader receives your letter. Don't wait to receive a reply! Initiative is appreciated and conveys enthusiasm.

Networking

Some of your best career contacts may be right under your nose. Your uncle, your doctor, the person who cuts your hair all have one thing in common: they are part of your network, and they may be able to introduce you to people they know who work in the career field you're interested in. Networking is an essential ingredient of any career-building strategy. Identify a dozen of your family, neighborhood professional, and personal contacts you know best. Ask them to give you the names of three people they know who work in the particular field you are interested in. Approach them on how you should introduce yourself. Oftentimes your friend or colleague will offer to pave the way by calling or writing a letter of introduction.

Send each of your new contacts a package containing a cover letter describing your career goals and a list of the companies you want to work for. Follow up with a telephone call. It's a good idea to practice your phone technique in advance. You may want to write out a short script that is concise and says exactly what you want to get across. Ask your contact if he or she knows anyone in any of the fields in which you are looking for a job.

It's important to understand the kind of employee each type of organization seeks. For example, unless you have years of relevant experience and prestigious university degrees, public multinationals are difficult to break into. Some government agencies are extremely competitive also. For example, only one in ninety-three applicants to the State Department gets a job there. The Peace Corps, contrary to the popular image, accepts people of all ages—if they have skills that are needed in developing nations. Two adventurous friends of the authors, Ralph and Jean, married for fifty years, got Peace Corps assignments together in Tonga. Businesses generally want you to spend a year or so in the United States, learning what the company is all about, before sending you trekking to an overseas post. Educational and private voluntary organizations often require special contacts to smooth the way to an international job.

Ask friends, and friends of friends, for ideas. What companies might hire for overseas work? Ask the local reference librarian for leads. Then start to zero in on them.

Identifying Contacts

Once you evaluate in what general field you want to get a job, ask yourself several questions. Where do people in this field get together? How am I going to meet them? Who are the wheeler-dealers in the field? The answers are simple. The logical place where practitioners in a field get together is at their annual conferences or trade shows. How do you find out where these are? Go to the library and read the trade journals. Often there are a number of conferences: pick one that's close to you.

So you go to the annual conference. Now how do you meet the right people? This is where skimming those trade journals comes in handy. You jot down the names of some of the people who have published articles you enjoyed. You look for them on the program. Then you talk to them afterward. ("I really enjoyed your article on community development projects in Papua New Guinea. . . .") You ask them to suggest leads for you to follow. ("Where should I begin to look for a job that will lead to an overseas posting in community development?")

Informational Interviews

Once you have obtained the names of prospective companies and organizations, do your homework. Learn about your target's products or services, its competition, and its organizational structure. The Internet will be a great boon to you here. Virtually every company or organization has a website. You may find the names of individuals strategically placed in the organization in which you are interested. Next, call that person using the most appropriate name in your network and say something like, "Ms. Wilson, Dr. Brown suggested I contact you. He said you might be able to help me in the field."

The Interview

There are three phases to any interview: preparation, the interview, and follow-up.

Preparation

Learn something about the person you are going to interview, and something about his or her organization. Jot down a few questions to ask ("What job do you think someone of my background might qualify for?" "What's the current job market in this area?" "Can you suggest some people I could talk to about the field?")

Interview

Listen carefully, be polite and at ease. Focus on the interview. Don't look out the window or appear bored or distracted. Be ready to leave without delay when you get a signal that the contact person wants to get back to his or her work.

Follow-Up

Do send a thank-you note. Your contact person didn't have to take time out of his or her schedule to see you. If you get a job as a result of another contact the person gave you, note it and thank the person for that, too.

Lois wanted a job in the Washington, D.C., area that would involve working with Asian refugees. She didn't know what kind of job her background would qualify her for, much less where to apply for a job. One of her professors gave Lois the name of a Mr. Chin, a prominent person in the field of intercultural communication who worked in the Washington area. Lois called, used her professor's name, and asked for an interview. The professor was known to Mr. Chin, and Chin readily agreed to a meeting. During the meeting, Mr. Chin went out of his way to suggest several general categories of jobs for which Lois would be qualified. Then he suggested several agencies she might want to contact. Lois went to the one that looked most interesting, told the director that Mr. Chin had suggested she contact them, and a week later Lois was working for the agency.

Job Interviews

Many books have been written about successful techniques for job interviews. (They are similar to those used in informational interviews.) Some good sources are listed below. Read one or two of them, then go for it! There are many international jobs out there for foreign language aficionados.

For More Information

In addition to the wealth of resources on the Internet, these books will give you more detailed information on job searches.

Copeland, Joyce H. *Where the Jobs Are*. Third edition. Franklin Lakes, NJ: The Career Press, Inc., 2000.

Lowell, Stephanie. *Careers in the Nonprofit Sector*. Cambridge, MA: Harvard Business School, 2000.

Echaore-McDavid, Susan. *Career Opportunities in Law Enforcement, Security and Protective Services*. Checkmark Books, 2000.

Krannich, Ronald L. *Dynamic Resumes: 101 Great Examples and Tips for Success!* Fourth edition. Impact Publications, 1999.

Electronic Canadian Job-Search Resources

http://campusaccess.com
   This site is a fully searchable on-line version of the publication *Student Employment Guide* and many other job-related resources.

http://canadianjobsearch.com
   The Canadian Association of Career Educators and Employers offers on-line versions of *Experience Magazine* and *Career Options Magazine*, as well as a searchable *Directory of Canadian Internships*.

State Offices of Volunteerism

ALABAMA
Governor's Office on State and Community Service
100 North Union Street
Montgomery, AL 36130
www.goncs.state.al.us

ALASKA
Alaska State Community Service Commission
Department of Education
333 West Fourth Avenue, Suite 220
Anchorage, AK 99501

ARIZONA
Office of the Governor
Division of Volunteerism
1700 West Washington, Suite 101
Phoenix, AZ 85007

ARKANSAS
Arkansas Department of Human Services
Donaghey Plaza South
P.O. Box 1437, Slot 1300
Little Rock, AR 72203
www.state.ar.us/dhs/adov

CALIFORNIA
California Commission on Service
1110 K Street, Suite 210
Sacramento, CA 95814
www.cilts.ca.gov

COLORADO
Governor's Commission on Community Service
1391 North Speer Boulevard, Suite 600
Denver, CO 80204

CONNECTICUT
Connecticut Commission on National and Community Service
Department of Higher Education
61 Woodland Street
Hartford, CT 06105

DELAWARE
Division of State Service Centers
1901 North Du Pont Highway
Charles Debnam Building
New Castle, DE 19720

DISTRICT OF COLUMBIA
Department of Employment Services
500 C Street NW, Room 600
Washington, DC 20001

FLORIDA
Florida Commission on Community Services
444 Appleyard Drive
Tallahassee, FL 32304
www.fccs.org

GEORGIA
Georgia Department of Community Affairs
60 Executive Park South NE
Atlanta, GA 30329

HAWAII
State Volunteer Services
Office of the Governor
State Capitol, Room 415
Honolulu, HI 96813

IDAHO
Idaho Commission for National and Community Service
1299 North Orchard, Suite 110
Boise, ID 83706

ILLINOIS
Governor's Hometown Awards Program
Department of Commerce and Community Affairs
620 East Adams Street
Springfield, IL 62701
www.commerce.st.il.us/communities

INDIANA
Indiana Commission on Community Service and Volunteerism
302 West Washington Street, Room E220
Indianapolis, IN 46204
www.state.IN.US/iccsv

IOWA
Governor's Office for Volunteers
State Capitol
Des Moines, IA 50319

KANSAS
Kansas Commission on National and Community Service
601 Woodson, Box 320
Lecompton, KS 66050

KENTUCKY
Kentucky Commission on Community Volunteerism and Service
275 East Main Street, Mail Stop 3W-C
Frankfort, KY 40621
http://volunteerky.state.ky.us

LOUISIANA
Louisiana Service Commission
263 Third Street, Suite 610-B
Baton Rouge, LA 70801
www.crt.state.la.us/laserve

MAINE
Maine Commission for Community Service
Maine State Planning Office
138 State Street
38 State House Station
Augusta, ME 04333

MARYLAND
Governor's Office on Service and Volunteerism
State Office Center
300 West Preston Street, Room 608
Baltimore, MD 21201

MASSACHUSETTS
Massachusetts Service Alliance
120 Boylston Street, Second Floor
Boston, MA 02116
www.msalliance.org

MICHIGAN
Michigan Community Service Commission
George Romney Building, Fourth Floor
111 South Capitol Avenue
Lansing, MI 48913
www.state.mi.us/career/mcse

MINNESOTA
Minnesota Office of Citizenship and Volunteer Services
117 University Avenue
Ford Building, Third Floor
St. Paul, MN 55155
www.mocvs.state.mn.us

MISSISSIPPI
Mississippi Commission for Volunteer Services
3825 Ridgewood Road
Jackson, MS 39211
www.mcvs.org

MISSOURI
Missouri Community Service Commission
770 Truman State Office Building, P.O. Box 118
Jefferson City, MO 65102
www.movolunteers.org

NEBRASKA
Nebraska Volunteer Service Commission
State Capitol, Sixth Floor West
P.O. Box 98927
Lincoln, NE 68509
www.nol.org/home/nvsc

NEVADA
Nevada Commission for National and Community Service, Inc.
90 North Maine Street, Suite 204
Fallon, NV 89406
www.ncncs.com

NEW HAMPSHIRE
Office of Volunteerism
124 Glade Path
P.O. Box 2120
Hampton, NH 03843
www.state.nh.us/das/volunteer

NEW JERSEY
Governor's Office of Volunteerism
225 West State Street
P.O.Box 456
Trenton, NJ 08625
www.state.nj.us/state/volunteerism

NEW MEXICO
Deputy for Administration
Office of the Governor
State Capitol, Room 400
Santa Fe, NM 87503
www.governor.state.nm.us

NEW YORK
New York State Commission on National and Community
    Services
40 North Pearl Street
Albany, NY 12243
www.nyscncs.org

NORTH CAROLINA
Governor's Office of Citizen and Community Services
116 West Jones Street
Raleigh, NC 27603
www.governor.st.nc.us/govoffice/citizen

NORTH DAKOTA
Center for New Americans
Lutheran Social Services of North Dakota
1616 Capitol
Bismarck, ND 58501
and
720 Main Street
Fargo, ND 58102

OHIO
Governor's Community Service Council
51 North High Street, Suite 481
Columbus, OH 43215
www.state.oh.us/ohiogcsc

OKLAHOMA
Community Services Commission
505 Northeast Thirteenth
Oklahoma City, OK 73104
www.okamericorps.com

OREGON
Oregon's School-To-Work Career-Related Learning Program
155 Cottage Street NE, U30
Salem, OR 97301
www.oregonjobs.org/stw

PENNSYLVANIA
PennSERVE: Governor's Office of Citizen's Service
Labor and Industry Building, Room 1304
Seventh and Forster Street
Harrisburg, PA 17120

RHODE ISLAND
Volunteer Center of Rhode Island
168 Broad Street
Providence, RI 02903
www.volunteerri.org

SOUTH CAROLINA
Volunteer Services Liaison
Office of the Governor
1205 Pendleton Street
Columbia, SC 29201

SOUTH DAKOTA
Helpline Center
Volunteer Information Center
1000 West Avenue North, Suite 310
Sioux Falls, SD 57104

TENNESSEE
Tennessee Commission on National and Community Service
312 Eighth Avenue North, Twelfth Floor
William R. Snodgrass Tennessee Tower
Nashville, TN 37243

TEXAS
Texas Commission on Volunteerism and Community Service
P.O. Box 13385
Austin, TX 78711
www.txserve.org/txcus

UTAH
Utah Commission on Volunteers
1530 North Technology Way, Suite D-03
Orem, UT 84097
www.utahspromise.org

VERMONT
Vermont Commission on National and Community Service
National Life Building, Drawer 33
Montpelier, VT 05633
www.state.vt.us/cncs

VIRGINIA
Virginia Commission on National and Community Service
730 East Broad Street
Richmond, VA 23219
www.dss.state.va.us/community

WASHINGTON
Washington State Commission for National and Community
   Service
P.O. Box 43113
Olympia, WA 98504
www.wa.gov/wcncs

WEST VIRGINIA
West Virginia Commission for National and Community
   Service
State Capitol Complex
1900 Washington Street East
Charleston, WV 25305
www.connectwv.org

WISCONSIN
Department of Health and Family Services
Director of the Bureau of Community/Family Development
1 West Wilson Street
Madison, WI 53708
www.dhfs.st.wi.us

WYOMING
The Needs Inc. Volunteer Information Center
Community Service Connection
900 Central Avenue
Cheyenne, WY 82007

Volunteers in Canada

Volunteer Vancouver Center
#301 - 3102 Main Street
Vancouver, BC V5T 3G7
Canada
www.vancouver.volunteer.ca

This organization promotes volunteer participation and strengthens the voluntary sector. A young Canadian volunteer sums it up: "Why do I volunteer? A selfish motivation for personal training and the good feeling I get from helping people."

Volunteer Centre of Winnipeg
410 #5 Donald Street South
Winnipeg, MB R3L 2T4
Canada
www.volunteerwinnipeg.mb.ca

The focus of this group is fund-raising, volunteerism, and training.

Volunteer Opportunity Exchange
430 Gilmour Street
Ottawa, ON K2P 0R8
Canada
www.voe-reb.org

Get information on U.S. and Canadian internships and organizations for volunteers in a variety of fields, including business, medical, Canadian government, and working with children and the environment.

Employers of International Consultants

Advanced Technology Ventures (ATV)
485 Ramona Street, Suite 200
Palo Alto, CA 94301
www.atvcapitol.com

Adventist Development and Relief Agency International
12501 Old Columbia Pike
Silver Spring, MD 20904

The Asia Foundation
485 California Street, Fourteenth Floor
San Francisco, CA 94104
www.asiafoundation.org

Associates in Rural Development, Inc.
159 Bank Street, Third Floor
Burlington, VT 05401
www.ardinc.com/ardinc

Berger, Louis, International, Inc.
100 Halsted Street
East Orange, NJ 07019
www. engineering.usa.edu

Black and Veatch, Engineers-Architects
8400 Ward Parkway
P.O. Box 8405
Kansas City, MO 64114
www.bv.com

Catholic Relief Services
2099 West Fayette Street
Baltimore, MD 21201
www.catholicrelief.org

CARE-Cooperative
151 Ellis Street NE
Atlanta, GA 30303
www.care.org

Cooperative Housing Foundation (CHF)
8300 Colesville Road, Suite 420
Silver Spring, MD 20910
www.chfhq.org

Education Developmental Center
55 Chapel Street
Newton MA 02460
www.edu.org

Family Health International (FHI)
P.O. Box 13950
Research Triangle Park, NC 27709
www.fhi.org

Spanish Education Development Center
1840 Kalorama Road NW
Washington, DC 20009
www.atmar.com/sedl

Institute for Development Anthropology
99 Collier Street
P.O. Box 2207
Binghamton, NY 13902
www.devanth.org

International Executive Service Corps
Stamford Harbor Park
Stamford, CT 06902
www.iesc.or.cr

International Food Policy Research Institute
2033 K Street
Washington, DC 20006
www.ifpri.org

Helen Keller International, Inc.
90 West Street
New York, NY 10006
www.hki.org

Little, Arthur D., Inc.
25 Acorn Park
Cambridge, MA 02140
www.plastics-ctr.org

Nathan Associates Inc
2101 Wilson Boulevard
2 Colonial Place
Arlington, VA 22201
www.nathanassoc.com

National Academy of Science
2101 Constitution Avenue NW
Washington, DC 20418
www.nationalacademies.org

National Research Council
2101 Constitution Avenue NW
Washington, DC 20418
www.nas.edu/nrc

Parsons Brinckerhoff, Inc.
1 Penn Plaza
New York, NY 10119
www.pbworld.com

Pathfinder International
Nine Galen Street, Suite 217
Watertown, MA 02472
www.pathfind.org

People-to-People Health Foundation
Project Hope
Health Sciences Education Center
Millwood, VA 22646
www.projhope.org

Planning & Development Collaborative International
   (PADCO)
1025 Thomas Jefferson Street NW, Suite 170
Washington, DC 20007
www.padcoinc.com

Population Council
One Dag Hammarskjold Plaza
New York, NY 10017
www.popcouncil.org

Population Reference Bureau
1875 Connecticut Avenue NW, Suite 520
Washington, DC 20009
www.prb.org

Pragma International
7918 Jones Branch Drive
McLean, VA 22102

PriceWaterhouse Coopers LLP
1301 Avenue of the Americas
New York, NY 10019
www.pw.com

Research Triangle Institute
P.O. Box 12194
Research Triangle Park, NC 27709
www.rti.org

Save the Children Federation
54 Wilton Road
Westport, CT 06880
www.savethechildren.org

Tropical Research and Development
7001 Southwest Twenty-fourth Avenue
Gainesville, FL 32607
www.trd.com

United Nations Childrens Fund (UNICEF)
Three United Nations Plaza
New York, NY 10017
www.unicef.org

U.S. Fund for UNICEF
333 East Thirty-eighth Street
New York, NY 10016
www.unicef.org

Urban Institute
2100 M Street NW
Washington, DC 20037
www.urban.org

World Wildlife Fund
1250 Twenty-fourth Street NW
Washington, DC 20037
www.wwf.org

Trade Offices

Committee on Canada–U.S. Relations
c/o U.S. Chamber of Commerce
1615 H Street NW
Washington, DC 20062

Consulate Trade Offices are located in Cleveland, Ohio; Buffalo, New York; Princeton, New Jersey; and San Francisco and San Jose, California.

Cultural-Political Organizations

Association for Canadian Studies in the United States
1317 F Street NW, #920
Washington, DC 20004

U.S. Embassy in Ottawa
100 Wellington St.
Ottawa, ON K1P 5T1
Canada

Humanitarian Affairs–Canada
Canadian International Development Agency (CIDA)
200 Promenade du Portage
Hull, PQ K1A OG4
Canada

Consulates in the United States

U.N. MISSION, NEW YORK
885 Second Avenue, Fourteenth floor
New York, NY 10017

EMBASSY IN WASHINGTON, D.C.
501 Pennsylvania Avenue NW
Washington, DC 20001

CALIFORNIA
550 South Hope Street, Ninth Floor
Los Angeles, CA 90071

FLORIDA
200 South Biscayne Boulevard, #1600
Miami, FL 33131

GEORGIA
1 CNN Center, South Tower, #400
Atlanta, GA 30303

ILLINOIS
180 North Stetson Avenue, #2400
Chicago, IL 60601

MASSACHUSETTS
3 Copley Place, #400
Boston, MA 02116

MICHIGAN
600 Renaissance Center, #1100
Detroit, MI 48243

MINNESOTA
701 Fourth Avenue South, Ninth floor
Minneapolis, MN 55415

NEW YORK
3000 Marine Midland Center, Thirtieth Floor
Buffalo, NY 14203

1251 Avenue of the Americas
New York, NY 10020

TEXAS
750 North Saint Paul Street, #1700
Dallas, TX 75201

WASHINGTON
412 Plaza 600
Sixth and Stewart Streets
Seattle, WA 98101

About the Authors

H. Ned Seelye quit high school at the end of his junior year and hitchhiked to Mexico to seek his fortune. In two weeks his future became clear: it was zilch. He didn't know Spanish, had no work permit, had not a single marketable skill (couldn't even type), and didn't know anybody in Mexico. It was time for Plan B. Seelye entered college on the basis of entrance exams (what other basis was there?), became fluent in Spanish, and acquired some marketable skills. Seelye specialized in intercultural communication and educational research (mostly in developing countries) and lived almost twenty years abroad. His international career included projects in thirty countries in Europe, Africa, Asia, and Latin America. He held many positions of responsibility, including Illinois State Foreign Language Supervisor, Illinois State Director of Bilingual Education, CEO of International Resource Development, Inc. (a social science research firm in LaGrange, Illinois), Associate Professor of Sociology and Anthropology at George Williams College (Illinois), and Executive Director of the Spanish Education Development Center (Washington, D.C.). During his career he was active in the American Council on the Teaching of Foreign Languages, the National Association of Bilingual Educators, and Society for International Education Training and Research. Seelye is listed in *Who's Who in International Education* (1980) and received the National Association of Bilingual Education Pioneer in Bilingual Education Award in 1991. He lectured in more than a dozen educational centers abroad, including holding the senior Fulbright Hays lectureship at the Catholic University of Ecuador (Quito) in 1975 and afterward becoming the first American professor to receive a regular appointment by the university. He authored more than sixty articles in journals and chapters in books in the areas of cross-cultural testing, intercultural communication, curriculum development, and workplace productivity, and wrote six books besides this one, including three editions of perhaps his best-known book, *Teaching Culture*. When he suddenly died of a heart attack in Albuquerque, New Mexico, he was working on a sequel to *Between Cultures: Developing Self-Identity in a World of Diversity* with his coauthor, Jacqueline Wasilewski; it will be ready for publication next year.

J. Laurence Day joined the faculty of the Department of Communication Arts, University of West Florida, in 1988 after twenty-two years as professor at the William Allen White School of Journalism, University of Kansas. He earned B.A. and M.A. degrees at Brigham Young University and a Ph.D. at the University of Minnesota. Day has been a UPI correspondent in Latin America and a reporter and copyeditor for U.S. metropolitan newspapers. His career research interests include professionalization of Latin American journalists and international news flow, about which he has published extensively. He has won three senior Fulbright lectureships, taught at fifteen universities in Latin America, and conducted workshops for journalists in Africa and throughout Latin America and the Caribbean. He was on the team that produced the television documentaries "Giving Up the Canal," "A Campaign for Cuba," and "Cuba: The End of the Revolution." With H. Ned Seelye, he produced nine anti–drug abuse comic books that were published in English and Spanish and distributed nationwide to at-risk young people.

Marvalee Welch returned to college after a hiatus of several decades and earned a bachelor's degree *summa cum laude* at the University of West Florida in 1999. She received the Department of Communication Arts top scholar medal and was inducted into Kappa Tau Alpha national journalism honor society. Welch volunteered as a researcher and editorial associate for this edition.